Library of
Davidson College

SETTLEMENTS OF HOPE

Cultural Survival Report 31

SETTLEMENTS OF HOPE
An Account of Tibetan Refugees in Nepal

Ann Armbrecht Forbes

Cultural Survival, Inc.
Cambridge, Massachusetts

Cultural Survival, Inc.
11 Divinity Avenue
Cambridge, MA 02138
(617) 495-2562

©1989 by Cultural Survival, Inc. All rights reserved. No part of this book may be reproduced, stored in a retrieval system, or transcribed, in any form or by any means, electronic, mechanical, photocopying, recording, or otherwise, without the prior written permission of the publisher, Cultural Survival, Inc.

Printed in the United States of America
by Transcript Printing Company, Peterborough, NH 03458

Cultural Survival Report 31
The Cultural Survival Report is a continuation of the Occasional Paper series.

Library of Congress Cataloging-in-Publication Data
Forbes, Ann Armbrecht, 1962-
    Settlements of hope : an account of Tibetan refugees in Nepal / Ann Armbrecht Forbes.
       p.   cm. — (Cultural survival report : 31)
    Includes bibliographical references.
    ISBN 0-939521-45-8 : $19.95. — ISBN 0-939521-44-X (pbk.) : $10.00
    1. Tibetans—Nepal. 2. Refugees, Political—Nepal. 3. Refugees, Political—China—Tibet. 4. Nepal—Exiles. I. Title. II. Series.
    DS493.9.T53F67 1989
    305.8'95405496—dc20   89-37141
                                                                                           CIP

This book is dedicated to Tibetan children — the third generation of refugees — who are struggling to build their lives and culture in exile.

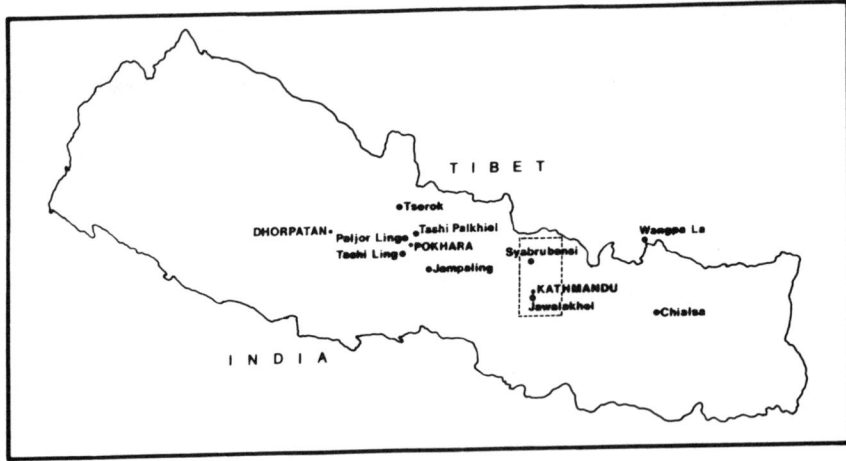

Nepal

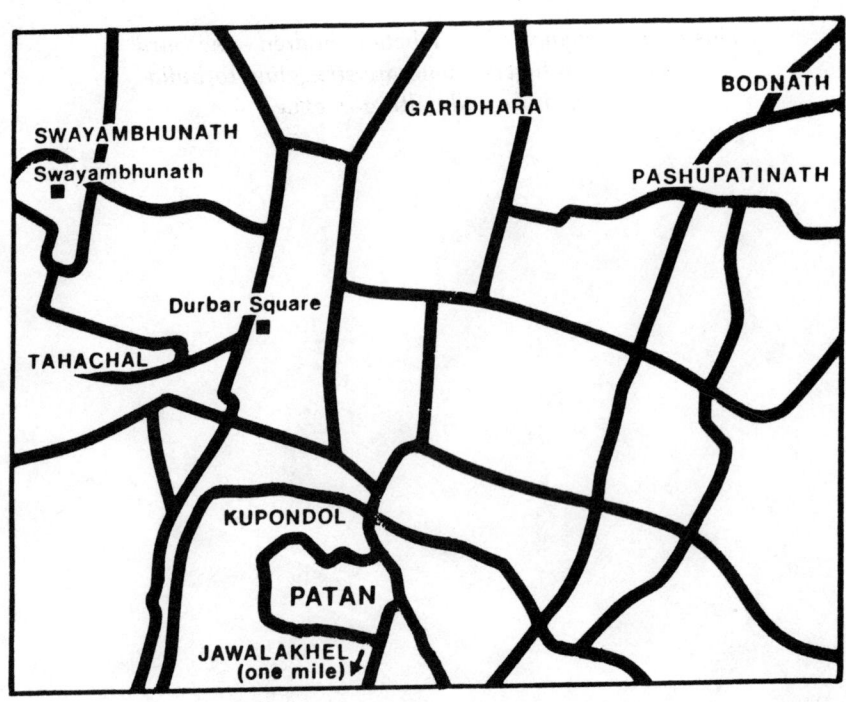

Detail of Kathmandu

Foreword

Adaptability is a quality that throughout their history has helped the Tibetans survive as a unique people. In their homeland even the environment presented a rigorous challenge, yet they happily took it in their stride.

Since the Chinese occupation of Tibet, which forcibly deprived Tibetans of the freedom to follow their traditional way of life, many of them have escaped to start anew. With all their possessions and sometimes their families left behind, faced with drastically different climatic conditions and unfamiliar customs, Tibetans have successfully reestablished communities in various settlements, particularly in India and Nepal. There, with a view to preserving their precious heritage, they have been able to maintain their cultural identity and freely practice their religion, while also benefiting from the advances of the modern world. In Nepal, especially, much of this success has been achieved by the people's own resourcefulness, private enterprise in the production and marketing of carpets significantly contributing to the welfare of the community.

While Ann Armbrecht Forbes was teaching Tibetan children in Nepal, she developed a great interest in the Tibetan refugees in that country and visited many of their settlements. Her book, *Settlements of Hope*, written as a result, describes the challenges facing Tibetans as refugees. The title is apt because in such settlements lie the hopes of a people whose very existence continues to be threatened in their own land.

THE DALAI LAMA

His Holiness the Dalai Lama
18 August 1989

Prologue

Throughout history foreigners who have encountered the people of Tibet have been profoundly moved by the Tibetan way of life, by the religious essence of the people and their simplicity and generosity. Even those who have only read of Tibet in books are caught up in the spell of these people who for centuries remained isolated on the roof of the world. Such foreigners are then left struggling to pinpoint the origin of the haunting influence that Tibet and its people exercise over them. Why Tibetans and not Cambodians, Ethiopians, Afghans, or any of the millions of other victims of conquest and destruction? Do Tibetans in fact hold the key to certain spiritual secrets, or is our curiosity piqued by the need to believe in those secrets?

The illusion that the people of Tibet held answers to unresolved issues in my own life certainly influenced my decision to spend time in their communities. I quickly discovered, however, that the Tibetans are, simply, people: they argue and fight and make mistakes; they are wrong as often as they are right; they disappoint as much as any Westerner. And yet I, too, was captivated by that haunting power, and found myself groping to explain it.

At the end of my research, I traveled to Dharmsala, India—the seat of the Tibetan government-in-exile—to interview the Dalai Lama; it was there, as I am sure Tibetans would have predicted, that the nature and origin of this mystery became clearer. As I entered the reception room where the Dalai Lama meets his visitors, His Holiness came forward to take my hand. As I moved to place a white scarf in his hands as a sign of respect, I dropped my notebook, and as I was reaching down to retrieve it he instead was reaching for my hand in greeting. He laughed—a deep, rich, captivating laugh, a laugh that seemed to have little to do with my actions or to anything else in particular. That laugh seemed to affirm that this — that is, life — was a game; it was to be taken seriously, of course, but it was a game nonetheless, and neither my blundering nor anyone else's was cause for worry. The Dalai Lama's laughter made me feel as if I'd known him all my life, as if he were an old and dear friend.

During the interview, I had to remind myself repeatedly that I was speaking with His Holiness the Dalai Lama of Tibet. This man was the reincarnation of a god, he was a *bodhisattva* who had relinquished the bliss of nirvana and returned to the suffering of *samsara* to lead all sentient beings to enlightenment. He had been proclaimed king of 6 million people at the age of two; he had waged a brief war against the largest nation in the world; he was a figure of inspiration throughout the world. Most important, he was the sole source of hope for the survival of the Tibetan nation and Tibetan culture. And yet, on this steamy afternoon in July, he spoke with a 24-year-old American as if this meeting were no less important than his encounters with worldwide religious and political leaders.

His humility, his simplicity, and his directness struck me as remarkable in a world leader. His emphasis on communication, on the need to "establish contact with others, and to communicate heart to heart" is a message that cuts across economic, religious, and national boundaries. It is a message the world must embrace if we are to correct our present course of self-destruction.

The Dalai Lama embodies the hopes and aspirations of the Tibetan people. The Tibetans have embraced his message wholeheartedly; they are now struggling in exile to preserve their community in order to keep that message of communication and honesty alive. The Tibetans' experience as refugees represents a sustained effort by a society to live by their leader's values of honesty, compassion, and simplicity. If Tibetan culture slips away, the world will not only lose a unique addition to its diverse stock of peoples, it will also lose a path that offers peace and preservation to a world torn apart by war and exploitation.

Acknowledgments

This project was made possible in part with the assistance from the Snow Lion Foundation in Nepal and the Office of Tibet in New York City. Far more important, however, has been the direct and indirect support and assistance provided by numerous individuals both in Nepal and in the United States.

First, I extend warm thanks to all the Tibetans who offered their time and energy to this project and who made my stay in Nepal such a rewarding one. My special thanks go to Lobsang Nyima and Tsering Dolkar for willingly opening their home to me, and to the other families across Nepal who unquestionably gave me housing.

The students and teachers of the Atisha and Mount Everest schools were responsible for turning a potentially lonely and frustrating 18 months into one of the richest periods of my life. This book is dedicated to them both as an expression of support for their struggle in exile and also as a small way of thanking them for the enthusiasm and openness with which they accepted me into their lives. I especially thank the principals of these schools, Tsering Dhundup and Sonam Tsering, for their interest in and support of my work and, more importantly, for their dedication and commitment to improving Tibetan education in Nepal. Tsering Dhundup was particularly helpful in translating my numerous tapes and in answering my even more prolific questions.

I also thank Rinchen Dharlo for his assistance both in Nepal and, more recently, in the United States. My greatest debt, however, is to Karma Tashi, without whom this book would perhaps have never taken shape. I thank him for his assistance in conducting interviews, for his careful reviewing of the final product, and, most especially, for his quiet and untiring support of me and my work in the Tibetan communities in Nepal.

A number of foreigners—Bill Robbins, Peter Tse, Tim Ferris, Kritin

Nathan, Moire Gowen, Nils Dauliere, and Mary Taylor—helped me through some of the more difficult times in Nepal by joining me for a run, a meal, a beer, or a long walk. I thank them all, and those left unmentioned, for their friendship. I especially thank John and Sally Davenport for providing nutritional, emotional, and spiritual support at those times when I needed it most.

Barbara Garner provided invaluable assistance in gathering much of the information in Nepal; I also thank her for her insightful comments on initial drafts of the manuscript and, in particular, for her company and good humor on our trip to Dhorpatan. I would also like to thank Gregory Prince for his comments on some of the earliest drafts of the manuscript and for his enthusiasm for the project from its inception. Jason Clay, Lester Anderson, and Warren Smith at Cultural Survival have also been very supportive of this project, and I especially thank Cultural Survival's editor, Leslie Baker, for bringing a fresh eye and many worthwhile suggestions to the final manuscript.

My mother, Calvert Armbrecht, valiantly tackled the grammatical challenges of the earliest drafts. Much more importantly, however, I thank her and my father for allowing all of their children the freedom to seek their own paths while ensuring that we had a home and a family to which we could always return. Finally, I thank my husband, Peter Forbes, for his wonderful companionship through every stage of this project. He constantly encouraged me to go just one step further and was at my side each time I set out to take that step. Most especially, I thank him for supporting me whether I actually arrive at my final destination or not.

Contents

Introduction   1

Part One   Exile
1   Flight   7
2   Freedom and Aid   17
3   The Limits of Aid   34

Part Two   Providing the Means
4   Carpets   43
5   Himalayan Exporters   60
6   Horse Traders and Entrepreneurs   66

Part Three   Preserving the Ideal
7   Prayer Wheels and Stupas   81
8   Conflicts   94
9   The Third Generation   102
10   The Community   118

Part Four   The Ideal and the Reality
11   The Ideal   129
12   The Economic Reality   133
13   The Political Reality   147

Epilogue   158

References   163

Introduction

In December of 1986, the Dalai Lama traveled to Bodh Gaya, the site where the Buddha achieved enlightenment in 500 B.C., to bestow the Kalachakra Initiation. More than 300,000 had traveled for days, crammed between boxes and people, to reach this sacred site in time to attend the largest Buddhist gathering of the century and to receive the blessing of the 14th reincarnation of Chenrezig, the Tibetan god of compassion—the Dalai Lama of Tibet.

A single dirt road winds its way through the impoverished village of Bodh Gaya. On this occasion, video tents, magic shows, and sidewalk stalls crowd into the normally sleepy roadway. Everything from Indian toilet paper to silver artifacts carried down from the Tibetan plateau could be found in the markets. The tea shops were jammed with people: carpet sellers, yak herders, restaurant owners, beggars, monks, Western dharma bums, and world travelers. There were Bhutanese with barely enough money to get to the border of Bhutan, Ladakhis who had been walking for weeks, Germans, Sherpas, and Americans. Most prominent, however, were the Tibetans.

The gathering at Bodh Gaya was the largest collection of Tibetans since the flight of the Dalai Lama from his homeland in 1959. Under the temporary relaxation of Chinese rule, thousands of Tibetans were able to leave Tibet for the first time in order to see and be blessed by the Dalai Lama at least once before their death. Families separated during the Tibetan uprising in 1959 were united at Bodh Gaya for the first time in 27 years. Young boys and girls raised in a Communist society laid eyes on that leader whom they had worshiped only from afar, while others, born into the world as exiles, heard firsthand accounts of the tragedies that their people had undergone. New reports of the Chinese destruction in Tibet were passed on and exchanged with stories of the refugees' lives in exile.

Refugees planned visits to Tibet; those in Tibet discussed ways of spending time in India. And everyone shared dreams of a future when the refugees, led by the Dalai Lama, would return to a freed Tibet.

*   *   *   *   *

The third night of the ceremony at Bodh Gaya fell on a full moon. The full moon is a very auspicious time for Buddhists; on this day, while sitting under the Bodhi tree, the Buddha reached enlightenment. Each month, when the moon is full, the karma of all actions, both good and bad, is doubled. And so, as the hot sun dipped behind the hazy Gangetic plain, the pilgrims flocked to the site of the original bodhi tree.

On this night the huge stone temple, built to commemorate the Buddha's achievement, towered against the dark sky. The moon shone down on the throngs pulsing around the base. A dull chorus of "Om Mani Padme Hum" rose from the mass of people. Lights flickered everywhere as young monks, old women, and teenage boys and girls intently placed and lit candles on the stone walls. They put sticks of incense into cracks in the walls and poured melted butter into the thousands of butter lamps. Others prostrated for hours on wooden platforms, chanting constantly, their hands and knees wrapped in padded cloth. The waves of prayers chanted by large clusters of monks gathered around the base of the *stupa* (shrine) resonated against the stone temple, and the air was heavy with the thick smell of burning butter. A gentle orange glow lifted up into the sky.

The enclosure was alive with a palpable sensation of power created by the concentration of so much faith, by the physical manifestations of that faith. The chanting, the candles, the offerings of food heaped in a huge pile in front of the stupa — all of it arising from this faith. A spiritual force radiated from the enclosure with a purity and a fullness that is very rarely found in the modern world.

This connection, this bond with the sacred, is the single most important quality in Tibetan culture and, in turn, in Tibetan national identity. This sense of the spirit, which is embodied in the Dalai Lama, has strengthened the Tibetan community and enabled it to remain united despite the devastation of the Tibetan homeland by the Chinese Communists and the subtle encroachment of Western values since the Tibetans' arrival in exile.

*   *   *   *   *

Tibetans scattered throughout the world gathered together at Bodh Gaya; they expressed their support of the Dalai Lama and their desire to regain independence. They donated money to Tibetan monasteries and prayed for the long life of their leader. In these feelings of patriotism and spirituality, it was difficult to distinguish refugees living in India from those in Nepal, Switzerland, or the United States. Individual differences do exist, however. Because of circumstances unique to Nepal, the refugees' experiences in that country are unlike those of the refugees in India, Bhutan, or Canada. Tibetan leaders in Nepal felt it was important that this experience be recorded, that their story be told. They were concerned that the history of their resettlement, which until now has existed in the memories of older Tibetans and in scattered reports, would be lost forever as these people die and the memories are forgotten. For this reason, Rinchen Dharlo, Karma, Tashi Phuntsok, and scores of other Tibetans in Nepal took the time to recount their experiences since leaving their homeland and supported my inquiries into the past 27 years of exile in Nepal.

The story of the Tibetan resettlement in Nepal, however, is told not only to provide the Tibetans with a record of their past. The account of the Tibetans' experience is significant because their efforts have been, for the most part, successful. Unlike other refugee groups whose communities are increasingly characterized by violence, suicide attempts, and cultural fragmentation, the Tibetans' story is largely marked by cultural integrity, economic success, and a call for nonviolent efforts to regain independence. Together with the assistance of foreigners, Tibetan leaders are working to create a path by which the refugees can culturally, politically, and economically enter the modern world: a way by which they can survive as Tibetans in the twentieth century.

And yet, Tibetan children born in Nepal and India are third-generation refugees. These children are the first generation to have experienced the world only as exiles. The central theme in their identity is that they are homeless; the primary responsibilities they inherit are preserving the integrity of their culture and regaining control of their homeland — a land in which they have never lived. The numbers of such children have increased dramatically since World War II. Palestinians are born daily into a war in the Holy Land, Vietnamese are being raised in corrugated tin huts in Hong Kong, and Nicaraguans are being educated in the jungles of Honduras and the streets of Miami. These children are breaking new ground; they have few examples to follow as they struggle to balance their loyalties to their homeland with the pressures and opportunities of the modern world.

The Tibetans' story is told with the hope that it sheds light on this process of carving out a path that is both traditional and modern, a path where choosing to participate in the twentieth century does not necessarily entail sacrificing the uniqueness of one's traditional beliefs. By focusing on the particularly intense experience of refugees, this account describes a process that all people everywhere are undergoing, a process of change and growth and loss: a process of cultural survival.

Part One

Exile

Who told you that you were permitted to settle in?
who told you that this or that would last forever?
did no one ever tell you that you will never in the world
feel at home in the world.
— *Stanislaw Baranczak*

Thus shall ye think of all this fleeting world:
A star at dawn, a bubble in the stream,
A flash of lightning in a summer cloud,
A flickering of lights, a phantom, and a dream.
— *Tathagata*

Chapter 1

Flight

Three miles south of Kathmandu in an area called Jawalakhel is a rambling old palace with dark rooms and low ceilings. It is a remnant of a previous age, of a time when the powerful Rana family had ruled Nepal with an iron hand, claiming to be the "hereditary" prime ministers while keeping the king of Nepal in his own palace under house arrest. Old buildings such as this, three or four stories tall and surrounded by high, stone walls, are scattered throughout the Kathmandu valley. After 1951 when, with the help of India, the Rana rule was brought to an end and King Tribhuvan assumed sovereign powers, many of these Rana palaces were vacated and later became grazing grounds for sheep, housing for foreigners, and offices for foreign missions, foundations, and government ministries.

In February 1986 Tashi Phuntsok, the manager of a Tibetan government-in-exile carpet export factory, greeted me warmly in his office on the second floor of this same Rana Palace. The white paint was chipping and the walls were overgrown with vines. The Western formality of Tashi's appearance seemed out of place in this run-down old palace. After handling several brief business matters, Tashi made himself comfortable on the couch across from me. As we sipped our tea, he described his arrival in Nepal 27 years ago.

Tashi is one of the 10,000 Tibetan refugees who have settled in Nepal. He attended a small Tibetan day school in the hills south of Mount Everest until the fifth grade. After serving as a translator for Swiss health workers in the village dispensary, Tashi worked as an accountant for the carpet weaving center. Then, due to his proficiency in English and his willingness to learn, Swiss aid workers sent him to study formal accounting in England. He is now manager of one of the two exporting companies run by the Tibetan government-in-exile and owns one of the largest private carpet exporting factories in Nepal. His English is flawless, and he appears confident and at ease with his responsibilities of exporting 18,000 square meters of carpets each year and acting as a leader for the Tibetan community. His circumstances, he explained, have not always been this secure.

At the age of four, Tashi was sent to a village monastery near his home in Ting'gri, on the western border of Tibet. The following year, just as the warm weather approached, parents and relatives began arriving at the monastery and, with no explanations, removing their children. One day Tashi's father arrived; he quickly gathered Tashi's few belongings and together they set out at a rapid pace for their village. Rumors had been spreading that the Chinese army was approaching the villages north of Ting'gri, and Tashi's father realized their time was running out.

Several months earlier, the villagers of Ting'gri had heard on All India Radio of an uprising in Lhasa against the Chinese and of the flight of the Dalai Lama from the Norbu Lingka, his summer palace in Lhasa. A messenger from the village immediately set out by horseback for the nearest base of the Tibetan Resistance Army, Four Rivers Six Ranges, to offer the support of the men of Ting'gri. The men made preparations to leave to join the fight against the Chinese forces. The messenger returned several days later, however, with the news that the Chinese had swiftly crushed the Tibetan national movement. The Tibetans had no hope, he said. The messenger also brought word of the Dalai Lama's safe arrival in India. Since the flight of His Holiness, he reported, Tibetans throughout Tibet had been leaving their homes, their fields, and their possessions, and crossing the Himayala Mountains to join their leader in exile.

Tashi arrived home to find his mother and his older brothers burying bundles of treasures in a large hole dug behind their house. Ancient, hand-painted *thankhas* (cloth paintings), large wooden bowls lined with intricately carved silver, rectangular silver belt buckles, and turquoise and coral earrings, rings, and necklaces all went into the ground.

Bewildered by his father's abrupt actions and exhausted from their journey, Tashi fell asleep expecting to wake up in the morning to go tend the yak and sheep with his brother. To his surprise, in the middle of the night he was awakened by a slamming door and the muffled whispers of his parents. In the distance he heard gunshots. Tashi's parents quickly bundled him and his younger sister into heavy wool clothing and strapped them to their backs. Candles of neighbors also fleeing the Chinese flickered in the distance and sporadic gunfire continued to shatter the silence of the night. Tashi's parents set out toward the south—south because that was where the candles of other villagers led, south because they knew another land lay beyond the barrier of the Himalaya, and south because they had heard the Dalai Lama had gone in that direction on his flight from Lhasa.

The small group traveled throughout the night, stopping only briefly to rest and eat small portions of their limited supply of *tsampa* (roasted barley flour), which can be eaten dry and uncooked, and hard blocks of yak cheese. As morning dawned, his parents led Tashi and his sister into a dark, overgrown cave and told them not to leave until they returned. His parents then sneaked back to their house to fetch the two older sons and as many supplies as they could carry. They returned to the cave late in the day, collected their children, and set out across the southernmost edge of the windswept and barren Tibetan plateau. To escape detection by the Chinese army, the family slept during the day and traveled by night, following an established trade route south from Ting'gri. Their rests became shorter and shorter as they heard, or imagined they heard, gunshots in the distance; soon they did not dare to stop long enough even to boil water for tea.

On the fifth day, Tashi and his family climbed the steep rise to the Nang Pa, a pass nearly 19,000 feet up in the Himalaya Mountains, near Mount Everest. Tashi fought his way through waist-deep snow, struggling to keep his balance against the icy winds that whipped down from Sagarmartha; his parents helped him across deep crevasses without a rope, as they followed a trail of blood made by wounds on the feet of the yaks. When they finally reached the summit of the pass, Tashi and his family stood ready to enter a world of which they knew nothing. They had never seen a car or an airplane. They had never heard of World War I or World War II, of the Soviet Union or the United States. They had never traveled on a paved road and had never used electricity. It was 1959.

*   *   *   *   *

Tashi and his family were but six among the flood of 100,000 Tibetans (out of a total population of 6 million) who eventually fled Tibet to become refugees. Few of them knew any more about the world than Tashi did; all that these exhausted and disoriented Tibetans knew—and hoped—was that their leader, the Dalai Lama, would guide them through their country's most devastating tragedy—the invasion of the Chinese.

At the time of the Chinese invasion Tibet was materially one of the most isolated and undeveloped countries in the world. Life on the barren, windswept Tibetan plateau was hard and the weather severe; the food staples were tsampa, dried yak meat, and butter salt tea. Rice was a

In 1959, 100,000 Tibetans fled through the high passes of the Himalaya Mountains into India, Nepal, and a life of exile. They followed their leader, the 14th Dalai Lama of Tibet, who has reestablished a Tibetan government-in-exile in Dharmsala, India.

©Ann Forbes

luxury and fruits and vegetables were almost unheard-of. Most Tibetans were illiterate peasants who farmed a few acres of land or lived as nomads. They kept warm during the long, bitter winters by wearing heavy wool clothing, gathering around fires of yak dung (the only fuel in this treeless country), and drinking 50 cups of butter salt tea a day. Tibetans say that while standing on this plateau, which lies at an average elevation of 13,000 feet, one's face, in the sunshine, might be blistering from the heat while one's feet, in the shade, are suffering from frostbite.

Technologically, Tibet was far behind the Western world. It had no electricity, no automobiles, and few paved roads. In their isolation, however, Tibet's people had developed a highly sophisticated philosophical tradition, based on the tenets of Buddhism, that rivaled those of the world's most enlightened civilizations. The philosophy of the dharma—"the light of heaven," as one Westerner put it—permeates every realm of their lives, from the day-to-day activities of a Tibetan peasant to the diagnosis of a Tibetan doctor to the political decisions of their leaders. "Spiritually," writes the Dalai Lama,

> Tibet was very rich. Apart from Buddhism which took deep roots in the country, many great ancient sciences, arts, and ideas from her neighboring countries found their way into Tibet, which gradually became a melting pot of great Asian civilizations. . . . We took Tibet's spiritual greatness for granted and almost ignored our material backwardness. (Dalai Lama 1980:25)

There were at least 4,000 major temples and monasteries in Tibet, and 30 percent of its male population were monks. "The monasteries became the seats of the national industry, the inner perfection of minds and souls through education and contemplation" (Thurman 1985). The largest of these monasteries served as the educational institutions of the country, where monks studied complex philosophical texts and scriptures; the most advanced monks worked toward the highest degree of Geshe, which was only awarded after 20 years of intensive training. Not all monks were scholars, however; many could barely write their names. Yet they were not seeking the knowledge of this world, but were concerned with mastering a more encompassing wisdom to reach an eternal peace: they sought enlightenment and escape from the continual rebirth of samsara. "We seek a permanent happiness," a Tibetan *Rinpoche* (a religious teacher, an incarnation) observed, "and we know that the material world is not the answer."

Vajrayana Buddhism is a profound and philosophically rigorous school in which the practitioner works to achieve enlightenment in a single lifetime. At the time of the Chinese invasion, Tibet was the only nation that continued to practice this branch of Buddhism in its pure form. In conjunction with the tenets of Vajrayana Buddhism, Tibet had a highly developed medical tradition that provided unique and insightful interpretations into the causes of illness.

For the rest of the world Tibet was a land enveloped in a cloak of mystery. The country was ruled by a living god, the Dalai Lama, and romanticized as "Shangri-la," the lost paradise that will survive the destruction of the world. Adventurers dreamed up schemes to get through the closed doors of Tibet and be the first to lay foreign eyes on the golden city of Lhasa and the magnificent structure of the Potala. Tales of monks flying across the plateau a foot above the ground and heating their bodies in subarctic temperatures through their religious powers filtered down off the roof of the world. Outsiders who did succeed in reaching Tibet said that this culture represented

> the last citadel of all that present-day humanity is longing for, either because it has been lost or not yet been realized or because it is in danger of disappearing from human sight: the stability of a tradition, which has its roots not only in a historical or cultural past, but within the innermost being of man. (Lama Govinda 1970:xi)

The 14th Dalai Lama was not destined to lead his 6 million followers to enlightenment in isolation on the roof of the world, however, nor were Westerners meant to retain their romantic dreams of Shangri-la. In 1950 the blood of the Communist revolution in China spilled out over the peaceful land of Tibet and the reality of the twentieth century struck. In 1950 the Chinese came to "liberate" the Tibetan peasants, destroying the cycle of traditional life in Tibet. Families were broken up, monks were separated from their teachers, and portions of the land, which had been left untouched out of respect for the gods, were opened for exploitation.

The Chinese Communists confiscated all private property. They forced Tibetan children to go to Peking to study in Chinese schools, and they initiated what were known as *thamzings*, or "revolutionary struggle" sessions. A district leader in Tibet who tried to work with the Chinese leaders described these sessions as:

> diabolically cruel criticism meetings where children were made to accuse their parents of imaginary crimes; where farmers were made to denounce and beat up landlords; where pupils were made to degrade their teachers; where every shred of dignity in a man was torn to pieces by his own people, his own children and his own loved ones. Aged lamas were made to fornicate with whores in public, and often the accused was beaten, spat, and urinated on. Every act of degradation was heaped upon him — and it killed him in more ways than one. When a man was through with a Thamzing session, no one ever spoke of him again. He was no martyr for the people, because the people had killed him. His death lay in the hands of those who should have honored and remembered him; but in their guilt, the people tried to forget him and the shameful part they had played in his degradation. (Norbu 1979:122)

The Chinese Communists closed the medical college in Lhasa and imprisoned Tibetan doctors. They shut down Tibetan schools, and forbade the practice of all traditional Tibetan dances, songs, and religious ceremonies.

The situation in Tibet reached a climax on 10 March 1959, after China announced new repressive measures against Buddhism and indicated that it was planning to take the Dalai Lama to Peking against his will. Tibetans in Lhasa rose up in arms. While Tibetans clashed with the Chinese on the streets of Lhasa, Tibet's 24-year-old leader finally decided that he could serve his nation best free of Chinese control. The Dalai Lama escaped in secrecy during the night of March 17, and, under the protection of guerrilla soldiers from Kham, fled into India and a life of exile.

Word of the Dalai Lama's flight quickly spread across the Tibetan plateau. Masses of Tibetans such as Tashi and his family — nomads, farmers, landowners, monks, and government officials — packed up what they could carry and set out to follow their leader through the high mountain passes of the Himalayas and down into the neighboring countries of India, Bhutan, Nepal, and Sikkim.

*　　*　　*　　*　　*

Having finally reached the top of the 19,000-foot pass that marks the border between Nepal and Tibet, Tashi and his family began the climb down into the Khumbu Valley and Namche Bazaar. Namche Bazaar is a village known to the Western world as the home of the Sherpas, now famous for their mountaineering and entrepreneurial skills. The village, a seven-day walk from the nearest road, sprawls out across a treeless ridge of carved terraces; even though it lies at 11,000 feet, it is dwarfed by the surrounding snow-covered peaks. Once planted with potatoes, the terraces are now used primarily as campsites for the many trekking groups stopping overnight on their way to Mount Everest and the Khumbu region. The shops are jammed with goods either left over from mountaineering expeditions or carried up in 80-kilo loads by barefoot Nepalese porters: Cadbury chocolate bars, biscuits from India, bottles of beer and soda, wool sweaters, and toilet paper all sell for four to seven times the price they fetch in Kathmandu. Hot showers can be purchased for ten times the cost of a bed. The central part of the town is lined with two-, three-, and four-story glass-windowed tea shops, which sport elaborate signs in English advertising the delectable chocolate cake and apple pie that can be bought inside. The villagers wear store-bought cotton clothes, down-filled parkas, and navy blue Chinese tennis shoes.

Compared to most remote Nepalese villages at this altitude, Namche Bazaar is extremely wealthy. Most communities have much smaller houses with one, or at the most two, stories and empty openings for windows. The children in these poorer villages run around in bare feet and worn-out cotton clothes, and their parents work long hours in tiny terraced fields to eke out a subsistence living. Even in the 1950s, Namche Bazaar, located on one of the primary trading routes to Tibet, was better off than most villages in Nepal. Despite this prosperity, however, the region always had a food deficit and a limited wood supply.

In 1959 a few Tibetans crossed the Nang Pa and traveled down into Thami, a smaller settlement west of Namche. To the Sherpas, these Tibetans were nothing unusual. The Nang Pa was an active trading route between Nepal and Tibet, and many Sherpas traveled north to Ting'gri on business and encountered Tibetans with herds of yak laden with salt and wool. Other Sherpas crossed the Himalayas to receive the blessings of Tushig Rinpoche, a lama revered by Sherpa and Tibetan alike, in Dza-rong, his monastery on the northern side of Mount Everest. Soon, however, the trickle of refugees became a flood and the Sherpas realized the Tibetans were not there simply to buy wheat and rice. A Tibetan guessed that there were approximately 3,000 Sherpas living in the area at this time; he estimated that 7,000 Tibetans passed through the Nang Pa and into the Khumbu Valley.

Initially the Tibetans were scattered, pitching their black yak hair tents on any available space and grazing their yak and sheep wherever there was grass. Many refugees arriving in India had had to travel months from their homes in the interior regions of Tibet before they finally reached freedom. They carried only their children and enough tsampa to last the journey; they had no blankets, no cups, no clothing. The Tibetan expression "We escaped from Tibet some with our bowls, some without even our bowls" describes the sum of the average refugee's possessions at this time. The majority of the refugees arriving in Namche Bazaar and other villages along Nepal's northern border, however, came from the southwestern region of Tibet, just beyond the Himalaya Mountains. Often these Tibetans were close enough to their homes to sneak back into Tibet to collect livestock and valuables that they had left behind.

Tushig Rinpoche, who also had fled Tibet, was able to distribute some food to the refugees from donations he received from local Sherpas. A handful of refugees obtained odd jobs working in the fields or carrying manure. The majority, however, began to sell their belongings—jewelry, clothing, silver belt buckles, and livestock—in order to buy food. Many Tibetans recall the tremendous relief they felt upon discovering that they could get money from selling these goods. But, because at that time they understood neither the value of the currency nor of the goods, jewelry worth a fortune was traded for as little as several bags of rice. A wealthy Tibetan carpet factory owner estimated that the value of the jewels his family sold in those early days would now equal the value of his entire business.

The Sherpas themselves had migrated from Tibet approximately 450 years earlier; they practiced the same religion as the Tibetans, their language was similar, and they had traded through the Nang Pa for years. Even so, the Sherpas were overwhelmed, and far from overjoyed, at the sudden influx of Tibetans and their livestock; any feelings of benevolence they had felt toward their northern neighbors were now severely strained. The sudden increase in the population of Namche created a drastic shortage of grains and other staples and magnified the already existing pressures on limited amounts of firewood and grazing land. The crisis was exacerbated by the closing down of the Tibetan border, which blocked the primary source of income for the Khumbu Valley. Soon, every time a Tibetan tried to set up a tent, a Sherpa arrived to claim the land as his; when the refugees grazed their livestock, the Sherpas cried out for them to get out of their fields. In other areas of Nepal, the Tibetans were called *Bhote,* the Nepali word for "Tibetan." Although this name in itself is not derogatory, the Nepalese meant it as an insult and used it frequently to remind the refugees that they were second-class citizens, paupers leeching off someone else's land.

Although potatoes, rice, and vegetables were scarce in Namche, the refugees soon had plenty of meat from slaughtering those animals that had succumbed to the lower altitude. As long as they were able to get some food, the Tibetans did not bother to make any long-term plans or to find employment; they were certain it would only be a matter of weeks — or, at the most, months — before they would return to their homes. In villages scattered across Nepal, refugees passed their days playing mahjongg and their nights folk dancing. From an outsider's perspective, this carefree behavior from refugees who had just lost everything seems a bit surprising. "Yes," agreed a 60-year-old Tibetan,

> We were sad because we had lost our country and we had nothing, but we had suffered under the hands of the Chinese for a while and had escaped. We were very happy to be in a free country. Everyone had clothes to wear and any essential necessities. As long as you have something to eat you can always dance, sing and play.

Every Wednesday during this initial period, in honor of the Dalai Lama's birthday, the refugees would climb to an auspicious site high on a hill to continue the tradition of "Lha So." For this particular prayer, Tibetans must form a group and chant in unison for 15 to 20 minutes. As the prayers draw to a close, the refugees raise offerings of tsampa to the gods three times, chanting a deep, drawn-out "Soooooooo" that echoes out across the valley. After the third round, they throw the tsampa into the air, shouting *"Lha So Gyal!"* ("Victory to the Gods!")

Gradually the refugees in Namche began to run out of goods to sell. Weeks, months, a year passed and they still had no word of the Dalai Lama's return to Tibet. Fighting their fear of the rumored heat of the lower altitudes and silencing their hope for a rapid return home, those families that were strong enough to travel began to pack up their few belongings and head south to Kathmandu and to India in hopes of finding a better life closer to the Dalai Lama. Several families preferred to return to life in Tibet under Chinese rule rather than struggle as beggars and second-class citizens in a foreign country. Those staying in the Khumbu Valley set about devising a means of earning a livelihood for what they still thought would only be a short stay — maybe a few years, at the most — in exile.

Chapter 2

Freedom and Aid

> I had heard many strange and wonderful things about life in Nepal, that the opportunities were very great. When I was a student in India, I was told by a relative living in Nepal that if I ever should visit, I should go to the Royal Hotel in Kathmandu and at the desk ask for the owner, Mr. Boris, who, I was told, would offer me a pastry.
>
> — *Tibetan schoolteacher, Nepal*

The inhabitants of Nepal, the country into which Tashi and his family entered, knew little more about events occurring in the world than did the refugees. The only Hindu monarchy in the world, Nepal had only opened its doors to foreigners in 1951. In 1959, this tiny country, sandwiched between two powerful neighbors—India to the south and Communist China to the north—was struggling to modernize and develop itself as rapidly as possible to ensure that it did not suffer the same fate as Tibet.

Kathmandu, the capital and the only true city in the country, was a small, medieval village in 1960. Even in 1986, after 35 years of Western influence and modernization, the sights and sounds of this now sprawling city seemed to belong to another era. Men in white jodhpur pants and women in colorful printed saris carry woven baskets overflowing with tomatoes, cucumbers, onions, and carrots from their fields to spread out on the ground under the shadows of intricately carved two- and three-story wooden pagodas. Large stone tigers, lions or elephants guard the entryways to the stone courtyards of the homes of Nepal's former royal families, and scrawny dogs sniff along the alleyways for food. Dirt roads weave past small stone shrines that hold Ganesh, the elephant man, or Shiva and Kali. The statues are covered with yellow flower petals and red *tika* powder left by Nepali worshippers performing their early-morning *pujas*. Elsewhere wizened old men and women and laughing, raven-haired girls dressed in saris bathe and wash clothes under water pouring from the mouths of stone dragons. Outside the Kathmandu valley, men and women laden with tremendous loads of water, goods, and produce travel on treacherous mountain paths and terrace the steep mountain slopes to plant wheat, corn, and potatoes. They spend their entire lives in remote villages in isolated valleys, and they worship their leader, King Birenda, as an incarnation of the Hindu god Vishnu.

For its size, 54,362 square meters, approximately the size of Illinois or New York, Nepal is one of the most geographically diverse countries in the world. The highest mountains in the world, six of which stand more than 26,000 feet above sea level, fall within the country's northern boundary. The land drops dramatically and rapidly from these peaks through the densely populated and heavily cultivated middle hills of Nepal to the tropical jungle of the Terai, where it joins the northern rim of the Gangetic plain at 600 feet above sea level.

In the early 1960s the population of Nepal was approximately 9.4 million. It was estimated that two out of every three children died and that the average life expectancy was between 25 and 30 years. The GNP was and still is one of the lowest in the world, and the literacy rate was 6 percent (Harris 1973:xvi). Nepal's natural resources include a rapidly dwindling lumber supply and the untapped hydroelectric power of the raging mountain rivers flowing off the Himalayas. Its most important resource, however, has proved to be the mountains that were thought to pose such a problem for its development. These mountains have attracted travelers and mountaineers from around the world and have thus been an important source of highly valued foreign currency.

Nepal's application for acceptance in the United Nations was approved on 14 December 1955, and the United States and France officially opened embassies there in 1959. Nepal's foreign policy has emphasized the "theme of friendship and peaceful coexistence with all countries — within the framework of nonalignment and neutrality" (Harris 1973:xxvii). Since establishing international contacts, Nepal's leaders have sought to develop aid relations with as many countries as possible while carefully avoiding involvement in any political treaties that might force them to choose sides.

The Communist invasion of Tibet had far-reaching implications for the future of Nepal. In addition to the material hardships, the influx of Tibetan refugees seriously jeopardized the political neutrality the monarchy had struggled to maintain. Nepalese leaders were clearly aware of the danger posed by the refugees' presence that the Chinese Communists could launch a military invasion of Nepal (Harris 1973:319). A Tibetan explains:

> There is pressure from the Chinese side on His Majesty's Government of Nepal [not to recognize Tibetan refugees] because Tibetans staying as refugees becomes a thorn for the Chinese. The Chinese say there is no such thing as refugees, but the Nepalese government has issued cards that say so-and-so is a Tibetan refugee living in Nepal.

Caught between India to the south and a now-Communist China to the north, Nepal's primary concern was in maintaining her own sovereignty.

By 1987 Nepal still had not ratified the UN charter defining the term *refugee*, nor had it recognized the doctrine of the United Nations High Commissioner for Refugees (UNHCR), which holds that "no individual seeking asylum should be forced to return to that country." Although Nepal was thus not legally bound to grant asylum to Tibetans, and despite the dangers of accepting those whom the Chinese labeled as traitors, the Nepalese government — as did the Indian government — never forced Tibetans to return to their homeland.

Tibet's neighbors were willing to risk Chinese wrath because of the long-standing religious and economic connections among the Himalayan countries. For centuries Tibetans had traveled to Buddhist temples in India and Nepal, and Indians and Nepalese, in turn, had gone on pilgrimages to Mount Kailesh, the holy mountain of Tibet. Tibet had acquired the foundations of its culture from Indian scholars and, since the Muslim invasion of northern India in the 13th century, Tibet represented the last stronghold of Vajrayana Buddhism. Buddhists in India and Nepal considered the Dalai Lama to be their spiritual leader and would welcome him under any circumstances; non-Buddhists greeted him as a world religious leader who had suffered unjustly under the hands of the Chinese and was in need of help.

Tibet's neighbors were not the only ones to express concern for its exiled population. People around the world were captivated by their plight and intrigued by the story of these inhabitants of the once-forbidden Shangri-la. *Newsweek, Time,* and *Life* all ran cover stories on the Dalai Lama's escape, with photographs of the masses of destitute Tibetan peasants carrying all of their belongings in canvas sacks slung over their shoulders. Many individuals otherwise uninterested in international aid or development work donated money, medicine, or second-hand clothing to assist the exiled peasants. International organizations immediately mobilized to distribute food, provide health care, and set up temporary camps. The residents of the countries that harbored the refugees were also malnourished, sick, and illiterate; they too could have used some international assistance. The undeniable mystique surrounding the Tibetan culture certainly explains

Twenty-five years later, Karma is a leader in the Tibetan community in Nepal. Heeding the advice of a lama, Karma turned down a foreigner's offer to send his two daughters to an English-medium school in India, instead choosing to keep them in the Tibetan schools in Nepal. ©Peter Forbes

much of the attention the refugees received. The sudden concentration on the Tibetans' predicament also illustrated a central paradox of disaster relief: disasters make news and, in heightened public awareness, attract money, food, and medicine to regions previously overlooked by donor dollars. Refugees are given food while those on whose land they are allowed to settle remain on the back pages and continue to go hungry.

*   *   *   *   *

Karma grew up in a nomad family in western Tibet. For several years his family had heard rumors of the arrival of the Chinese in eastern Tibet and of the increasingly repressive regulations imposed by the Communists. In 1959 they received news of the uprising in Lhasa and of the flight of the Dalai Lama. Finally, in March 1960, Karma's parents decided to leave Tibet. With pots, pans, and bundles of valuables strapped on the backs of several shaggy yaks, they and four other families set out along the trading route south to Nepal. They managed to avoid both the Chinese army and the Khampas who had been pillaging the area for several days, until they reached the southern peaks bordering Nepal.

Just as the sun climbed over the mountains, on the morning the group planned to cross the highest peaks, Karma noticed dust billowing up into the sky as if a storm were approaching. It was the Chinese army. Looking ahead, toward the final pass before freedom, Karma spotted Chinese sentries silhouetted against the gray sky, their jackets billowing in the icy wind, their rifles poised. Since other Chinese troops were approaching from the north, the fugitives had no choice but to continue south. Suddenly a heavy cloud of mist enveloped the ridge. A Chinese soldier holding a gun shouted out for the Tibetans to wait, saying that he would help them. Ignoring the cries, Wangdu, Karma's father, dragged his son up the final stretch of snow, through the last mountain pass, and down into the tiny Hindu kingdom of Nepal, and freedom.

After traveling south for several more days, Karma and his family arrived in Mustang, where a number of other Tibetans had gathered. They set up a temporary home in a cave, ate what little tsampa they had left, and drank Tibetan salt tea without its characteristic butter. Finally, one morning in early March, the first Westerner Karma had ever seen arrived in Mustang. Everyone gathered around this strange, light-haired man who offered them food and medicine; older refugees greeted him with full-length prostrations. With the help of his Sherpa assistants, the man explained that lots of free food and medicine were available farther south, where Tibetan settlements were being established.

The Khampa guerrillas, who had arrived in Mustang to set up a base for the Tibetan Resistance Army, listened skeptically. The fiercely independent Khampas warned that people who followed the stranger would lose contact with their families, their neighbors, their compatriots, and their leader. By going south, they said, the refugees would be betraying the Tibetan cause. By this time, however, the fugitives had run out of goods to sell; those who were still healthy scoured the land for food, and others lay dying from an unknown fever. The Khampas could offer nothing to ease their plight. Thus, ignoring the ominous predictions of the Khampa warriors as best they could, Karma's family joined a large group of Tibetans and headed south down the Kali Gandaki gorge to the town of Pokhara.

In Pokhara the distribution of aid had not yet been organized and, in the spring of 1962, Karma and his family again followed the advice of the Westerners and this time set out on foot for the Kathmandu Valley. The walk from Pokhara to Kathmandu passes through the lush tropical valley of the Trisuli River, which winds along the southern edge of the Himalayan foothills. Karma's family followed the well-traveled path through the river valley, seeking shade from the unrelenting sun under the banana and mango trees scattered along the riverbank; at night they slept in fields beside the trail. When they stopped for meals on the outskirts of villages, Karma was sent in to beg for maize or millet while his father boiled water for tea on fires built from whatever sticks Karma had been able to collect.

The refugees were utterly exhausted. They had crossed the world's highest mountain range and had lived on little more than tsampa and salt tea for more than a year. The extreme heat, the 10,000-foot altitude drop, their lack of immunities to local diseases, and their total psychological disorientation made them weak and vulnerable. At the end of the third day of their journey from Pokhara, Karma's mother fell sick with the fever that had killed many Tibetans in Mustang, and from which Tashi Dhundup and his father had only recently recovered. Her health rapidly deteriorated; soon Tashi's father had to carry her while the eight-year-old carried their few remaining pots and pans and their bedrolls.

In early December 1961, after traveling for more than a month on a journey that usually takes only 10 days, the family, dressed in the now-threadbare *chubbas* they had been wearing when they left their home a year and a half ago, crossed into the Kathmandu valley. This fertile plain, criss-crossed with terraced fields and rimmed by 10,000-foot-high hills, was once submerged by a huge lake. According to legend, Manjusri, the Tibetan Bodhisattva who carries a flaming sword of wisdom to cut through delusion and ignorance, slashed the ring of hills to drain the lake and thus provide land for settlement. A deep, rocky gorge where the cut was made still exists at the southern edge of the valley.

The legend continues that a lotus flower, an auspicious symbol in Buddhism because of its ability to find nourishment and grow so beautifully in murky, dirty water, was blooming in the lake before it was drained. Once the valley was formed, the ground rose up and the people built a temple commemorating the spot where the lotus had been growing. The temple, which is now one of the world's most sacred Buddhist sites, was named *Swayambhunath.* Immediately upon arriving in the Kathmandu valley, Karma and his family set out for this holy shrine.

Kathmandu was the largest city Karma had ever seen. The fields were cultivated and green, and mud brick houses with thatched roofs dotted the landscape; the city had stores where goods could be purchased, and cars traversed its streets. "A bus was the most impressive sight," Tashi recalls. "It was so big! And of course the two stupas were something great, something grand and precious." After a week at Swayambhunath, he and his family traveled across town to Boudha, another Buddhist stupa on the outskirts of Kathmandu. In Boudha, Wangdu went to a lama for advice on where he should take his destitute family. The lama performed "MO," a practice in which he rolls dice and, according to how the numbers correlate to certain sections in the scriptures, offers his counsel. This lama advised the family not to return to Mustang but rather to go "to a place not far from here where Tibetans are being settled."

Once again Karma and his family picked up their bundles and wool bedrolls, this time setting out for Jawalakhel, a small village on the southern edge of Kathmandu where land had been set aside by His Majesty's Government of Nepal for the Tibetan refugees. By Nepal's standards, Jawalakhel is now a fairly prosperous town: the streets are paved and lined with newly built square cement houses and small shops, and the roads are busy with trucks, bicycles, cars, and people. Wheat and corn fields have been planted in small plots tucked between houses, although for the most part, the fields have been replaced by buildings, roads, and the fenced-in yards that mark the homes of wealthier residents. When Karma arrived in 1962, however, there was not even a paved road connecting the village to the capital five miles away. Jawalakhel was nothing more than a series of narrow dirt paths winding their way past thatched bamboo or stone houses scattered amidst the terraced fields of wheat, rice, and corn.

On arriving in Jawalakhel at noon, Wangdu immediately sent Karma to stand in the long line of Tibetan and Nepali men, women, and children waiting in the hot sun to fill their containers with water. After several hours, Karma returned to his parents with just enough water to boil for tea. Later in the day, his family went to the small cluster of white tents where his father had been told they would receive assistance. Standing under the shadow of a flapping red flag with a large white cross, Karma's father provided the information needed for the yellow registration forms used by the Swiss to try to keep track of the refugees. The Swiss recorded their names, village of origin, occupations in Tibet, and number of family members. The workers gave the new arrivals a food ration of rice, flour, onion, cooking oil, *dhal* (lentils), and salt, for their first complete meal in one and a half years.

As the sun slipped behind the surrounding hills, brown from the dry winters of Kathmandu, Karma's family was led to a flat, dusty spot in a field crowded with dirty white canvas tents and shown where they could set up their own tent. The pungent smell of yak cheese and rancid butter hung heavily over the camp. Refugees were boiling water on wood fires in the low openings of their tents and eating tsampa carried down in sheepskin bags out of hand-made wooden bowls. New and old arrivals exchanged village and family names and shared news and stories. Unlike the settlement in Namche and other remote areas, the refugees gathering in Jawalakhel came from villages scattered throughout Tibet. These were the poorest refugees to enter the Kathmandu valley, and they had been directed immediately to Jawalakhel, where the only aid in the valley was being provided.

By the time Karma and his family arrived in the camp, a group of concerned foreigners had established a small crafts center to provide the refugees with a means to earn their livelihood instead of depending entirely on handouts. Karma's mother soon joined 15 other middle-aged and older women who gathered daily to weave traditional Tibetan woolen belts in a run-down brick building rented from a local Nepali. His father made knives and scissors for the workers in the center. In Tibet, blacksmiths were considered a low caste because they made the instruments of killing, but Wangdu said it did not bother him to do this work in exile; his blood did not change and the work had to be done. In these early days, Karma spent many hours waiting in line for water. Once that was collected, he and the other children were put to work digging latrine holes. On Saturdays these children would rise at two o'clock in the morning to climb the 10,000-foot-high hills on the southern edge of Jawalakhel, where they would work until three or four o'clock in the afternoon to gather the week's firewood. As in Namche Bazaar, whenever the refugees had any spare time, they would gather for games of mah-jongg and, arm in arm, dance into the early morning hours.

*   *   *   *   *

News of the Dalai Lama's disappearance on the evening of 10 March 1959 had quickly spread by radio; the world anxiously awaited word of his reappearance. Reporters raced to the northern hills of India, swamped down onto Kālimpang and scoured the hills for signs of the "god-king"'s entrance. After several weeks the Indian government received word of the Dalai Lama's imminent arrival in Tezpur, and Prime Minister Nehru immediately dispatched a group of Gurkha soldiers to escort the Tibetan leader on the last stretch of his journey.

On March 31, the Dalai Lama, weak with dysentery, crossed the unseen line into freedom. A newly built bamboo gate decorated with flowers welcomed him, and the Gurkha commander presented the traditional white scarf of greeting. The press corps, still waiting in Kālimpang—and thus the world—had to be patient. It was not until three weeks later, after an 18-day ride on horseback through Assam and several days of rest, that the press were able to get their photos (Avedon 1984:60).

The world had its eyes riveted on the Dalai Lama and the refugees entering India; any donations of food, money, medicine, or clothing were sent immediately to the Dalai Lama, who subsequently settled in the hills north of Delhi, in Dharmsala. Meanwhile, the 20,000 refugees streaming across the border of Nepal were overlooked by the headlines and thus missed out on much of the aid. The Dalai Lama himself was overwhelmed with trying to organize assistance for the Tibetans flowing into India; even if he had had any provisions to offer, the communication between India and Nepal delayed word for some time on the refugees remaining in the Hindu country. Although the Nepalese government was willing to accept Tibetans, the monarchy did not have the resources or the international connections that India did and could offer little material relief to the refugees.

In 1961, the only existing welfare organization in Nepal was a small group composed primarily of members of the royal family. Called *Para Pakar*, this organization ran an orphanage and oversaw the cremation and burial of the dead. "They were doing good work," a foreigner later explained. "But they were medieval. They had no international connections, no audit, and financially, they were very irresponsible." Approximately one thousand foreigners were living in Nepal at this time, working in the diplomatic and aid missions that were slowly opening around the Kathmandu valley. In 1961, however, the founders of these organizations were still busy trying to adjust to life in Nepal and acquaint themselves with the country's most critical problems; none of them were equipped to meet the overwhelming needs of the Tibetan refugees.

Father Marshall Moran, a Jesuit priest who first came to Nepal in 1955, was one of these foreigners: "Nothing was being done before April 1960."

> There was no Red Cross or any other group helping the Tibetans. They were arriving by the hundreds and were under a tree here, under a tree there. They gravitated to Boudha and Swayambhu with their dirty black tents. They had never lived in a house in their lives, 90 percent were nomads. They were a menace to Kathmandu, diseased people and dirty and they were dying, in the morning they would be found dead by the road.

A renowned wireless radio buff, Father Moran was allowed to open the first English boarding school in exchange for the assurance that he would not force the Hindu students to convert to Christianity. As did most foreigners at the time, Father Moran recognized the tremendous health hazard the refugees created in Nepal, and he foresaw the Nepalese government's reluctance to assist them. He also realized that his familiarity with the customs of Nepal, his connections with government officials, and his understanding of the language could help to minimize the conflicts between foreign aid workers and the bureaucratic government of Nepal.

Calling on Nepal's international community to assist him in his efforts, the Jesuit formed the Nepal International Tibetan Refugee Relief Committee, known as "NITRRC" or, simply, "Father Moran's committee."

Foreigners, dismayed by the sudden influx of Tibetans and concerned about their economic, social, and political impacts on the fragile Nepalese economy, joined the committee. They held their first meeting on 7 April 1960 at the Royal Hotel in Kathmandu. Over pastries and tea provided by the hotel's proprietor, the infamous Russian Boris Lissanovitch, who was also a member of the committee, the members decided that NITRRC would be a temporary organization whose goal would be "to collect, administer, and disburse funds and relief on behalf of Tibetan refugees in Nepal" (NITRRC 1960). The committee kicked off its fundraising efforts at an Easter party sponsored by Americans living in Nepal; with the money raised, its members got down to business.

Another foreigner who found himself drawn from his regular surveying work to assist the refugees was the Swiss geologist Toni Hagen, who began trying to secure large-scale assistance from international organizations. He first contacted Prime Minister B.P. Koirela and Home Minister Surya Prasad Upadhya of Nepal on 6 January 1960. In a follow-up letter to the home minister, dated January 8, he described the crisis at hand:

> Although it is difficult (due to lack of communication and support) to assess the exact number of Tibetan refugees in Nepal, it is estimated that between 20,000 and 30,000 might have crossed the border into Nepal. By reasons of their accustomed environment they are so far crowded in the northern valleys.... The scope of the problem is illustrated by the fact that according to the information of my Sherpas ... the Tibetan refugees outnumber the local Sherpa population in the Khumbu two to one. There is no need to mention that it is as well in the interest of His Majesty's Government of Nepal to do something about the refugees. Otherwise, unrest and trouble will be inevitable and might thus create a very delicate situation for the country.

Hagen outlined a program that would provide immediate emergency relief while working toward a long-term solution of integrating the refugees into the Nepalese economy. The Nepal Home Ministry approved of Hagen's proposal and commissioned him to raise the funds needed to finance the project. Hagen first appealed to those closest to home: the Swiss Office for Technical Assistance and "Schweizer Auslanhilfe," two Swiss organizations with offices in Nepal. Both groups were reluctant to provide assistance until they had further clarification of the conditions of the refugees. The report eventually sent to Schweizer Auslanhilfe by its representative in Nepal, however, was extremely negative and highly unsupportive of the refugees' predicament:

> It is difficult to understand why Tibetans have fled; only the big landlords and lamas have been in danger. Indeed, the farmers and laborers have today under Chinese occupation a better living than before under the Dalai

Lama. This explains the high percentage of monks who are predominantly Charlatans amongst the refugees.

The report continued by describing the Tibetan refugees as mostly lazy monks and landlords who were unsuitable for regular work and resettlement (Froesch, quoted in Hagen 1969).

One might easily imagine the exchange on which the information for the report was based. The cultural differences were of such a huge magnitude and, given both the Tibetans' lack of comprehension and trust and the foreigners' lack of understanding of the internal nuances of the Tibetan community, the distortions and inaccuracies of the report are not at all surprising.

Regardless of the constraints on collecting the information, the Swiss were shocked with the conclusions of the report, which disputed all the descriptions they had received from Hagen. Since they had no other firsthand information by which to disprove the document, the two organizations refused to have anything to do with the refugees. The International Committee for Red Cross (ICRC), which had immediately sanctioned SFr 40,000 for emergency relief, also became hesitant and requested more information before embarking on a large-scale relief program. In May 1960, the Red Cross sent an employee to Nepal on a two-month fact-finding mission. The subsequent report simply supported the previous negative impression.

Father Moran remarked that during the first year, problems and disagreements did arise between certain foreigners and some of the Tibetan leaders. "The Tibetans have tremendous aristocratic levels of who's who. The official types did not want to get their hands dirty, they wore fancy clothes, and they were not willing to cooperate with our committee." Those refugees with whom the foreigners spoke had to be brave enough to volunteer to talk to strangers or clever enough to realize it might be beneficial to do so; thus the reports received in Switzerland were most likely based on encounters with the more visible refugees described by Father Moran. Questionnaires filled out by the Swiss document that, in fact, all economic levels were represented in the refugee population: there were landowners and wealthy businessmen, and also peasants, nomads, and tenant farmers.

Despite various foreigners' interpretations of the refugees' plight, the majority of Tibetans in Nepal were starving and sick. Their situation at this time was later summed up in a 1975 report for the UNHCR:

> Many, especially women and children, died on the way, or soon after arrival. Those who survived the grueling trek over the rugged 16,000 foot Himalayan passes were starving and utterly exhausted. None could speak the ... language, nor could their hosts remember Tibetan.... Unaccustomed to

Cultural Survival

the hot climate and low altitude, the majority developed skin diseases and gastric disorders. All needed food and shelter, and most needed medical care. (Holburn, quoted in Gombo 1975)

Lacking the connections of a long-established relief organization, Father Moran's committee was unable to meet the overwhelming demand for assistance; it was critical that a large aid group step in to assume responsibility. Hagen persevered until, with the help of Dr. Lindt, the United Nations High Commissioner for Refugees, he procured donations from Australia, England, and the West German Bishop's Conference. In late 1960, these funds were transferred to the ICRC. As its directors gradually realized the magnitude of the crisis, the ICRC assumed the primary responsibility for organizing and financing assistance to the Tibetans during the crucial initial phase. Hagen was appointed chief of ICRC's relief program in Nepal and was given the green light to commence large-scale operations.

The first challenge in developing a viable long-term assistance plan was to determine the scope of the Tibetan migration into Nepal and the actual nature of the refugees' situation. Conditions for the Tibetans in the Kathmandu valley were bad, yet these people at least were accessible. Most Tibetans in Nepal, however, were scattered in the mountains along the northern border, weeks away from any contact. Nepali education officers in Kathmandu established radio contact with schoolteachers all over Nepal to get an estimate of how many refugees had entered the country. Lobsang Gelek, the first representative of the Dalai Lama in Nepal, sent men to the police checkpoints located at entrances to the Kathmandu valley to register incoming Tibetans and to press them for comments on conditions in the border region.

The only way to find out what was actually going on, however, was to trek out to these areas, some as far away as two to three weeks from the capital. Luckily, there was the perfect volunteer for this work: Peter Aufschnaiter, an Austrian who had escaped a World War II internment camp in Dehra Dun, India, with Austrian mountaineer Heinrich Harrer. After fleeing across the Himalayas, the two had spent the next seven years traveling in Tibet and working in Lhasa — experiences that Harrer describes in his book, *Seven Years in Tibet*. Not only was Aufschnaiter fluent in Tibetan and familiar with the Himalaya Mountains, but many of the refugees remembered him from the time he had passed through their villages on his way to Lhasa. With the assistance of Sherpas, he hiked up to the border areas and determined roughly how many Tibetans were there, where they had settled, and the condition of the settlements.

In addition to allowing the Tibetans into the country, the Nepalese government offered one of the only resources it had to offer: land, at no or very little cost. ICRC used this land to establish what were to be temporary settlements, located in four areas: Chialsa, in Solu Khumbu to the east of Kathmandu; Hyanja or Tashi Palkheil, near Pokhara in central Nepal; Dhorpatan, in the western part of the country; and Jawalakhel, on the southern edge of Kathmandu. Twenty-nine years later, these and other "temporary settlements" still exist, continuing to be home for approximately half of the refugees living in Nepal.

The refugees in Jawalakhel settled on the dry stretch of land provided by the Nepalese and continued to live as they had in Tibet. They slept and cooked in tents made to withstand the bitter winters of the Tibetan plateau. They wore heavy black wool robes that looked and smelled like the yaks from whose hair they were woven; they rarely bathed, and they ate meat that was rotten, hanging it raw from strings in their tents to dry. The altitude and cold of Tibet had protected them from the health hazards of such customs. The tropical 90-degree temperatures of Kathmandu in the summer had the opposite effect: latent germs suddenly came to life, people contracted illnesses for which they had no immunities, and disease ran rampant.

The Shanta Bhawan Hospital, which had been started by the United Mission to Nepal, was at that time the only hospital in the Kathmandu valley. Medical facilities were limited throughout Nepal and trained doctors extremely scarce; the Nepalese themselves were in desperate need of medical attention. The Tibetan situation, however, was far more critical. Faced with new germs, a new climate, new food, and a significantly lower altitude, the refugees were dying at an alarming rate. Every Tibetan family can describe the death of at least one family member during the first two years in exile. Many died of dysentery, tuberculosis, or some identifiable epidemic; others simply died from exhaustion and a loss of hope.

"Disease was the most difficult thing in the beginning," Father Moran recalls. "The people were dying off. They came down here with their filthy black tents. There were some really sick people. In one year they had every disease in the book." There was an epidemic of diptheria in Dhorpatan and the sick people were told by Swiss doctors—who were consequently fired—to walk two-and-a-half weeks to Kathmandu; half of them died on the way. Several Tibetans contracted anthrax, a disease common to sheep and cattle; because it is rarely transmitted to humans, the doctors did not recognize the illness until two or three people had died. And, because of their poor nutrition and close living quarters, the refugees were especially susceptible to tuberculosis, a disease still found in many refugee communities. To make matters worse, those who were not seriously ill did not seek medical attention promptly as they were advised, thus causing many otherwise curable problems to become quite serious.

At first the Tibetans did not visit the health clinics voluntarily; many were frightened and suspicious of the Western doctors and their medicine. The refugees preferred to be treated by their own doctors, or to suffer alone in silence. As they watched their compatriots and family members growing weaker and dying for no apparent reason, however, their attitudes changed.

Karma's mother, who had fallen ill on their trek east from Pokhara, had still not recovered by the time they arrived in Jawalakhel. Even after finally settling down, she continued to weaken. Finally, at her husband's insistence, she joined the long line of Tibetans in front of the dispensary, where people waited for hours under the hot sun. Working out of the rundown Rana Palace that now houses the offices of the carpet export factory, a Western doctor and nurse treated minor illnesses with free medicine donated by foreigners. Nurses picked up seriously ill patients in a van twice a week and took them to the Shanta Bhawan Hospital, where a section of beds had been reserved for the Tibetans.

Father Moran's committee helped the refugees build grass huts on the dusty strip of land across from the crafts center. Some of the women on Father Moran's committee collected the men together by the water spigots and cut, washed, and combed their long hair to get rid of bugs. Others instructed all of the refugees in the use of latrines. Aid workers distributed food rations of rice flour, oil, onions, powdered milk, and dhal, donated by the United States Agency for International Development (AID) to all families once or twice a day. These workers took this opportunity to explain the importance of a balanced diet to the refugees, whose staple foods in Tibet had been tsampa and dried yak meat. The Tibetans, many of whom had had fresh milk in Tibet, refused to take the powdered milk; their reluctance was magnified by rumors from India that the powder was responsible for the spread of tuberculosis. The Tibetan assistants had to chase after the refugees to make them drink it. Nurses repeatedly explained that saving and eating raw meat in this hot climate would only exacerbate illness, often to no avail. The foreigners tried to teach the Tibetans to wash their bowls instead of simply licking them clean, and they distributed spoons.

Because of Tibet's cold weather, most Tibetans rarely washed. Skin infections erupted from the rubbing of heavy clothing against dirty skin. Father Moran's committee bought lightweight denim material and had the tailors in the training center sew red cotton shirts and chubbas for the most needy cases. The clothing problem was solved once and for all through an eccentric scheme cooked up by Boris Lissanovitch, the owner of the Royal Hotel. Boris was planning a movie about the war between north and south China, and he chose the jungle in the Terai of southern Nepal as the perfect film location. He borrowed 200 elephants, built two entire villages of 20 to 30 huts each to be set on fire during the war, and purchased hundreds of lightweight Tibetan robes as costumes. The movie failed to materialize and the refugees in Jawalakhel did receive a new wardrobe—the unused costumes.

In November 1963, several weeks after the Tibetans had started to build their grass huts, Father Moran received a call from the local magistrate saying that he had 24 hours to get all of the refugees out of the Kathmandu valley. Stunned, Father Moran explained that this was impossible, that the refugees had nowhere else to go, that they had been given land and were slowly becoming settled. The official refused to discuss the issue. Since it was too late in the day to contact more sympathetic government officials, Father Moran decided he had no other choice but to obey the order.

The priest explained to the refugees that they would have to leave their homes temporarily because the area was to be deloused. "We made a big show of it and went through a lot of silly operations," he said. "I didn't dare tell them that the government said they had to get out." He instructed them to pack up enough belongings, including their tents, for a few days. The group trudged up through Jawalakhel to a flat, grassy area in front of what is now a zoo. "The following morning," Father Moran recalls,

> I went to the King's secretary and said, "This is empty land that they're staying on, no one was living there. We're doing you a favor and turning the refugees into law-abiding citizens. We're starting a new industry and bringing in foreign exchange. Then this hyena comes in and kicks them out! He's not helping anything, and he gave them no new place to go. Will you have the king call him and say let those people go back?" That afternoon, the magistrate called me to say there had been some mistake and that the refugees could return to their original settlement.

In light of the attention and tremendous amounts of aid that the Tibetans were receiving, tensions inevitably arose between the local Nepalese and the refugees. A villager approached Mr. Rana, the Nepali employed by the Swiss in Dhorpatan, and asked "Why is it only Tibetans who should get free milk? Our children are also hungry and weak." As Mr. Rana recalls, "Things were really difficult in the beginning. The local Nepalese were really very tough. They were not happy about having Tibetans resettle in Dhorpatan, not at all. I had to be a very good diplomat to solve this problem." Every project involved negotiations with the local residents. A Swiss worker in the settlement in Solu Khumbu explained,

> In a short span of time we brought quite a bit of money into a populated area and that created a lot of problems. The Sherpas would come in the middle of the night and cut off the water pipes to the Tibetan community. They did this simply to harm the Tibetans whom they thought were privileged people because they had more money and more support.

The initial aid was provided to the refugees by the International Committee for the Red Cross. ICRC was founded in 1859 by Jean Henri Dunant during the battle of Solferino in Italy as a "civilian medical corps to tend the wounded of both sides on the battlefield" (Shawcross 1985:101). After the Second World War, the organization's responsibilities expanded to include "care for the general population in time of war and other disaster" (Shawcross 1985:103). In its attempts to assist the needy in situations of war and "other disasters," conflicts inevitably arise over the allocation of aid. When confronted with so much need, how does one choose whom to accept and whom to turn away? Will there not always be someone else down the street or in the next village in as great or greater need? ICRC was specifically created to care for victims of disasters; the Nepalese were struggling, but they had not been forced from their country. The Tibetans, who were political refugees from a Communist invasion, were thus the recipients of the organization's goodwill.

Of course, the Nepalese objections could not be ignored. To ease the tension, Swiss field workers throughout Nepal provided villagers with good quality potato and wheat seeds, donated school materials and furniture, and provided medical care to local Nepalese as well as Tibetans. In Dhorpatan the Swiss gave 75 percent of the powdered milk to the Tibetans and 25 percent to Nepali school children. They built wooden bridges over deep gorges. In Solu Khumbu, the Swiss agreed to build an airstrip for the local community at Phaplu and to establish a dispensary that would be open to the public. In Kathmandu, Father Moran's committee gave surplus medicine to the then-fledgling Nepal Red Cross.

The local people also learned from the examples of the Tibetans and the Swiss. Nepalese had traditionally used porters to transport their loads; in certain regions, they followed the exiles' example and began transporting goods on horses. In Dhorpatan the Nepalese had only grown just enough potatoes to feed themselves; the region later became famous for these potatoes when the Swiss helped the refugees establish a transportation business with potatoes as the main commodity.

* * * * *

After their unexpected exodus from Tibet, the refugees suddenly found themselves homeless, landless, and stateless. Their roots to the land had been torn up, their legal position in the world called into question. Their very identities—their homes, families, occupations, and village names—had been destroyed; suddenly, they were beggars in a strange land, plagued by the loss of their past and the uncertainty and insecurity of their future.

The foreigners in Nepal played an instrumental role in guiding the refugees through their physical and material adjustment to a modern and alien world. These Westerners provided critical support in laying the foundation for the economic future of the refugees. They could do little, however, to help the Tibetans survive the acute psychological and spiritual trauma of their displacement. The framework through which the refugees had understood and found meaning in the world had been destroyed; only they could reconstruct their culture and fill this vacuum in a meaningful and enduring way.

Chapter 3

The Limits of Aid

Six hundred miles to the northwest of Kathmandu, Tashi Phuntsok, his family, and the 4,000 other refugees who had remained in Namche Bazaar continued to sell their belongings and kill their sick yak and sheep for food. They collected wood from nearby hillsides, fetched water from mountain streams and waited in long lines to receive the blessing of Tushig Rinpoche at his temporary home in a Sherpa monastery northwest of Namche. After five years in exile, this sense of impermanence still remained; they built homes quickly and sloppily because they were certain they would soon return home. Many refugees were reluctant to follow foreigners' advice and plant apple trees because it took them five years to bear fruit; those who did support such enterprises were condemned as having given up hope.

On deciding to flee their homes and their homeland, the refugees took steps that completely and irreparably altered the course of their lives. Life as they had known it for 10, 20, or 60 years was not, and would never again be, the same. As farmers and as nomads their lives were guided by the seasons; as monks, by the needs of the spirit:

> "In Tibet one is not hunted from morning to night with the calls of 'civilization,' " a visitor to Tibet in the 1950s observed. "Here one has time to occupy oneself with religion and to call one's soul one's own. Here it is religion which takes up most of the room in the life of the individual, as it did in the olden days in the west." (Harrer 1959:233)

Lama Govinda believed that the essence of this spirituality lay in Tibet's unusual landscape. He writes:

> Never have I experienced this [the experience of our essential timelessness] deeper than under the open skies of Tibet, in the vastness of its solitudes, the clarity of its atmosphere, the luminosity of its colors and the plastic, almost abstract, purity of its mountain forms. . . .
>
> At night the dark blue velvet curtain of the sky is drawn back and allows a view into the depth of the universe. The stars are seen as bright and near as if they were part of the landscape. One can see them come right down to the horizon and suddenly vanish with a flicker, as if a man with a lantern had disappeared around the next corner. The universe here is no more a mere concept or a pale abstraction but a matter of direct experience; and nobody thinks of time other than in terms of sun, moon, and stars. The celestial bodies govern the rhythm of life, and thus even time loses its negative aspect and becomes the almost tangible experience of the ever-present, ever-recurring, self-renewing *movement* that is the essence of all existence. (Govinda 1970:61)

These descriptions are certainly the romantic speculations of foreigners impressed by the striking contrasts with the rest of the world. Yet every traveler to Tibet inevitably comments on the landscape — its bleakness, its remoteness, its clarity of light. Whether Tibetans themselves refer to the landscape and its impact on their culture in the same terms as outsiders, in such a materially undeveloped country the environment was inevitably the most pervasive force in their lives. The landscape was the reality in which they had to eke out a living, and was thus inextricably linked with their understanding of what it was to be a Tibetan.

Unlike the vast emptiness of the Tibetan plateau, Nepal is crowded: people, animals, streams, mountains — and, at that time, forests — all vie for space within narrow, deep valleys. Differences between the landscapes were compounded for Tibetans by changes in their daily tasks. As free citizens in their own country, Tibetans had traveled and worked in wide, open spaces. Villagers had produced what they needed and had bartered for everything else. In Nepal, however, they had no means of production and had to depend on Nepalese currency to buy goods. In Nepal, they lived in tents on foreigners' land or rented out rooms in strangers' homes.

The Communist invasion fragmented families, the core of Tibetan society: some members stayed behind; many died from the arduous journey and the extreme altitude change; others, later in exile, were sent to school in India. Outside their extended families, Tibetans are slow to form friendships; they reserve judgment, waiting to extend overt signs of acceptance until a stranger has earned their respect. Once they establish relationships, they form deep bonds, but even then, they are unlikely to share personal thoughts with even their closest friends. There is even a Tibetan proverb that says "Don't tell your secrets even to the bearer [mother] of three sons."

The Tibetans in many of the border towns of northern Nepal were able to remain with other members of their villages. Refugees arriving in the Kathmandu valley and those entering India, however, suddenly found themselves thrust into crowds of strangers. Many lost contact with religious leaders from whom they had sought instruction, advice and solace, and the upheaval disrupted the rhythm of their daily rituals. Finally, their leader, who was king of the roof of the world, patriarch of one of the world's oldest philosophies, and their only source of hope, had too been forced to flee his country and settle as a refugee in a tiny village in the hills northwest of Delhi. The Dalai Lama was treated with respect by outsiders, but he was recognized as the legal leader of Tibet by only his loyal followers.

The refugees in the border areas of Nepal heard rumors that the Dalai Lama had arrived safely in India and that thousands of refugees had followed. They subsequently received occasional news of the Dalai Lama's work in India and of events in Tibet following their departure, but they had no way to confirm such information. Finally, on a bitter, snowy morning in early 1961, after the 14-day trek to the Khumbu region, a Tibetan wrapped in a sheepskin coat arrived in Namche Bazaar and announced that he brought a message from the Dalai Lama. Several thousand refugees huddled together in the snow-covered fields under the shadow of the Himalaya Mountains to listen while the stranger read the message written by their leader:

> Now we have come to the land of another people. Do not lose your heart. Do not be discouraged. Hope, hope is there. Keep good relations with the local people wherever you are. We may face some problems with communication—but try your best. Be friendly with your neighbors and, most importantly, stay with the Tibetan community.

Few focused on the meaning; most simply wept with relief and happiness on hearing the words of His Holiness, and with despair over the fate of their country. An elderly Tibetan remembers: "When these messages came we felt very happy simply because they were from the Dalai Lama. If we saw Tibetan newspapers, anything to do with Tibetans or Tibet we were very happy." The Dalai Lama recalls these messages:

> During the summer of '59 my immediate task was to somehow save the refugees . . . [to meet their food, clothing, and medical needs]. Then, with the little knowledge we possessed, we took it as our duty to tell these "fresh" refugees that it was not so easy to return to Tibet. "We will have to remain in India for a longer period than we expected," we said. "We will have to settle mentally as well as physically." (quoted in Avedon 1984:72)

A Tibetan newspaper, *Tibetan Freedom*, printed in Darjeeling, India, became the greatest source of information for refugees scattered in remote areas. Founded and written by the few Tibetans who knew enough English to translate articles into Tibetan, the paper reported on how many Tibetans were reaching India and where they were arriving, what aid was being distributed and by whom, and, most important, what the Dalai Lama was doing in India. For the first time the refugees in Nepal learned that the Dalai Lama had established a government-in-exile to oversee the resettlement of Tibetans and to work toward regaining control of their country. Through the paper they heard that in India work had been found building roads, food was being distributed, and schools were being established.

Tibetan Freedom opened lines of communication between the exiles and rejuvenated the optimism that had gradually dissipated as the days had stretched into months and years of exile. The paper helped reduce the spread of rumors concerning events in Tibet, and it described the work of a small band of Tibetan guerrillas that had established its headquarters in northwestern Nepal. Of most long-term significance, perhaps, the paper served as the foundation for the development of a sense of unity among the diverse group of Tibetan refugees now scattered across the Himalaya Mountains and slowly spreading throughout the world. And it provided a voice through which these Tibetans could begin to articulate their vision of a future when Tibet would again be ruled by the Dalai Lama.

In early spring of 1961, soon after the messenger's visit to Namche Bazaar, two Tibetan officials from Dharmsala arrived in Kathmandu to investigate the condition of refugees in Nepal. Their subsequent report described the near-famine conditions endured by the refugees dispersed along Nepal's remote border regions and recommended that the exile government become directly involved in assisting them. Shortly thereafter, formal communication lines were established among Tibetans in Nepal, and between those in India and those in Nepal with the establishment of the Tibetan Welfare Office, Ghangdan Khangsar, in Kathmandu. As a branch of the Ministry of Home Affairs in Dharmsala, this office was to be a liaison for the Tibetans, the aid organizations, and the government of Nepal. Most important, the office was to serve as the voice of the Dalai Lama in Nepal.

After providing for the material needs of the refugees, the primary long-term goal of the government-in-exile was to work toward regaining Tibetan independence. The Dalai Lama foresaw that achieving this goal would not only depend on maintaining a strong sense of Tibetan cultural and national identity; the Tibetan government could not simply return to its previous ways of ruling Tibet. In his opinion, the successful rule of Tibet in the modern world depended both on the establishment of a government based on democratic principles and on the active participation of a population capable of bringing Tibet into the twentieth century. In exile, the Dalai Lama immediately met with Tibetan leaders to draft the first constitution in the history of Tibet, an alternative to Chinese rule. He began to establish a framework within which the refugees could retain their sense of Tibetanness while also acquiring the skills and knowledge of the modern world.

In working toward the objective of returning to Tibet, the government-in-exile had to plan as if it would remain in exile for a long time. A government minister said, "The office did not think only of the short term. We had the hope of returning soon, but home affairs had to plan these camps with a very long-term view. The plans were made with the idea we would have to stay for a long period, but if we had the chance to return to Tibet, there would be no difficulty in leaving." Schools, monasteries, economic opportunities, and Tibetan settlements were the pillars from which this goal was to be pursued. Of these, Tibetan leaders saw the settlements as the central vehicle for transmitting Tibetan culture on to the next generation. "The Dalai Lama has said it is best for Tibetans to live in camps," a Tibetan monk commented, "because they can discuss Tibet and freedom amongst each other and pass this knowledge on to their children. If we separate, this will be forgotten, and there will be no chance of regaining Tibet's freedom." Exile government staff sent to manage the settlements in India and Nepal were instructed to "collect these people and keep them in one place, to try to preserve Tibetan identity, religion, and culture and to give an education to the children."

The international workers, who, according to a Tibetan report, were "mainly to help with economic and medical needs," also saw the camps as an integral part of the Tibetan resettlement scheme. They, however, felt the settlements were valuable as a way of simplifying the distribution of aid, as a step toward assimilation into the economic, social, and political life of Nepal. Their assistance in creating Tibetan settlements was based on the understanding that "these people should gain their livelihood based on a principle of self-responsibility; once the refugees have been provided with the necessary infrastructure, they are to look after themselves within the laws of the country." In letters and documents, the Swiss discussed their hope that after a certain period the government of Nepal would allow Tibetans to become Nepalese citizens. The question of Tibetan independence was not an idea they even considered at the time.

The Tibetans' experience as refugees is perhaps unique in that they set forth their own vision of the future so soon after arriving in exile. Because the Dalai Lama had their complete support, the respect of foreigners, and some resources of his own, people listened to and acted on his ideas. He, not foreign advisors, defined the context within which international assistance would be provided and set the priorities for how that aid should be utilized.

His independent stance did not always go over so well with the foreigners trying to offer assistance. Father Moran said he was unable to get any information on the activities of the Dalai Lama, his representative in Nepal, or anyone else. "They don't trust anybody to let you know what they think or what they want. Most of them had no wishes, they just wondered, What does the Dalai Lama want? and they'd do it. In those days they were really very, very simple."

The control assumed by the Dalai Lama seems to be one of the most critical factors in the Tibetans' success as refugees. Quickly filling the void created by their traumatic experience, he ensured the continuance of their culture and their traditional ways of life in the face of the twentieth century. He provided them with a choice: to enter the modern world as a member of Tibetan society or to enter it alone as an individual. Most Tibetans have chosen the former option.

Part Two

Providing the Means

In 1978 Khamsum Wangdu opened a private carpet weaving factory in Kathmandu, Nepal, where he employed Nepalese and Tibetan weavers. A Nepalese government official once asked him why, if, as he said, he did not make much profit from his factory, he continued to do business. Wangdu replied, "We are refugees . . . there are Tibetan refugees in India, Nepal, Switzerland, Japan. . . . It is His Holiness's wish that, wherever we are, we do a business that earns our living but doesn't take bread from the local people. For example, in Switzerland, many people are foresters; in Japan, Tibetans paint Buddhist paintings; in India, they sell sweaters. In Nepal, since wool is not used much by the local people, we use it in carpets, jackets, etcetera. If I put a tea shop somewhere, it would hamper the local people's business because it would compete with them, but using wool does not. Our basic aim is not to make a big profit but to make a living."

Chapter 4

Carpets

The entrance to the Jawalakhel Handicraft Center is marked by a small stone stupa. Brightly colored red, blue, and green prayer flags interspersed with faded tattered ones from previous years flap gently in the cool morning breeze of early November. Low murmurs of "Om Mani Padme Hum" slip from several bent-over older men and women who clutch their worn wooden prayer beads and shuffle around the stupa. Short-haired, mangy mutts sniff along the dirt path leading away from the stupa, looking for garbage and unwanted food, and men relieve themselves by the side of the road. Shouts, banging doors, and falling pots from the nearby brick settlement houses interrupt the peaceful, early-morning air; the muffled pounding of carpet weaving mallets begins.

Women light the stoves and begin boiling water for tea; young girls wash clothes or weave carpets; men perform the morning religious duties and help straighten up the houses. By eight o'clock, a breakfast of *chapatis* or left-over rice has been eaten, and the morning chores are completed. Houses are locked, and the settlement empties. A few teenage boys walk up the street to their jobs with a private carpet exporter; others wander off to open their own one-room carpet shops that line the road leading away from the settlement. The majority, however, simply cross the street and pass through the brick gate of the carpet factory for work.

Most of the 20- and 30-year-old men in the settlement, many of whom were educated in Tibetan schools in India, climb the steps to the offices located above the sales shop. Here they keep the accounts, manage the carpet production, and look after the needs of the workers. Older women

The Dalai Lama is the sole source of hope for the survival of the Tibetan nation and Tibetan culture. He serves as a model for the refugees as they struggle to survive as Tibetans in the twentieth century.

in chubbas, teenage girls wearing second-hand clothing from foreigners, and a handful of men enter the long, single-story weaving hall to the left of the offices.

Sunlight streaming through the barred windows casts long shadows from the eight-foot-high wooden looms across the floor of the weaving hall. The weavers take their places, sitting cross-legged in groups of two, three, and four on low benches behind the looms. Working simultaneously, they weave the wool through the vertical warp, carefully following the color code of the carpet design. The row complete, with a wooden mallet they beat down the iron rod holding the woolen knots in place, cut out the rod with scissors made in the factory, and start a new row. As they weave, the workers sing popular Hindi and English songs, tell jokes, and gossip.

Wangmo, a 20-year-old mother, has been weaving since she dropped out of school in the fifth grade. When her eight-month-old daughter was sick, Wangmo worried about her; when Wangmo is arguing with her husband, she dreams of leaving him behind and going to America. Usually, however, she simply concentrates on weaving as quickly as she can. The weavers take morning and afternoon tea breaks, and have an hour for a lunch of

With the initial assistance of foreigners, Tibetans began weaving carpets to earn a living in exile. Through the refugees' efforts, this traditional craft has evolved into a major industry in Nepal, bringing much-needed foreign currency into the country as well as providing the refugees with an enterprise that is uniquely Tibetan. Shown here is the weaving hall in the Jawalakhel handicraft center. ©Ann Forbes

rice and dhal in their homes across the street.

Next to the weaving hall stands another long, cement-floored brick building with barred windows. This hall houses the spinners and carders of the wool: toothless, wrinkled older women with long, gray braids and heavy wool chubbas who patiently roll the wool into balls day after day,

Cultural Survival 45

Tibetans in the government-in-exile factories are involved in all stages of carpet production, from spinning and dyeing the wool to exporting the final product to Europe. More often, private factory owners employ Nepalese weavers while they handle the management and sales of the carpets. ©Ann Forbes

chanting Tibetan prayers and smiling and nodding to the tourists tromping through with their cameras.

A long, L-shaped building stretches along the end of the compound. One end houses huge metal cauldrons used for washing and dyeing the wool, which is imported from Tibet and, more recently, from New Zealand and England. The other serves as the wool store, where the weavers pick up the wool they need for their carpets. Skeins of wool, washed, dyed, and spun, are heaped on shelves, in corners, and against the wall. On the roof, workers spread out freshly dyed blue, green, and tan wool to dry.

When the Tibetan refugees flooded into Nepal in 1959, most Nepalese hoped they would continue on into India. The refugees would not only compete for the country's limited food, land and water resources, they would also vie for the scarce employment opportunities. If the Tibetans created more employment opportunities, however, their reception would have been different. Toni Hagen, who was responsible for ICRC's assistance in Nepal from 1961 through 1962, played a central role in setting the Tibetans on a path toward economic self-sufficiency. ICRC was primarily interested in emergency relief work; from the very beginning, however, Hagen felt strongly that they should try to find a more permanent solution and that they should work to integrate the refugees into the Nepalese economy (Gombo 1975:156). Hagen established a carpentry center, organized tailoring classes, and started a poultry farm. These ventures were successful on a small scale, but the Tibetans would eventually begin competing with the Nepalese tradesmen for supplies and customers. A more stable niche for the refugees had to be found.

* * * * *

Gyatso is the carpet master for Sagarmatha Carpets, a private carpet factory in Boudha. He moved down from Chialsa, the settlement in Solu Khumbu, in 1985, and his gaunt face has a ruggedness that is no longer visible in the faces of many Tibetans raised in Kathmandu. He was born in Ting'gri in western Tibet. His father died when he was only eight and Gyatso had to go to work to help his mother support their family. He had always been interested in learning how to weave carpets and he dreamed of becoming a carpet master. At the age of 13 he apprenticed to a local master, and remained there until the invasion two years later.

Tibetans have been weaving carpets, a skill they borrowed from either the Middle East or Central Asia, for more than a century (Denwood, quoted in Gombo 1975:96). In Shigatse, one of the three largest towns in Tibet, carpet weaving was a lucrative industry before the Chinese invasion, probably because the town was on the trading route from Lhasa to Kathmandu. In most of Tibet, however, carpet weaving remained a folk art and the hand-woven carpets were considered a luxury item that only wealthy landowners and businessmen could afford.

A good carpet weaver was considered an artist in Tibet: just as the paintings of a well-known painter are easily recognized, the carpets of an accomplished weaver are easily identified. "To weave a carpet you really have to put your energy and thought into it," Gyatso said. "It is not something that can be taught." In Tibet, he wove intricately designed carpets from his own patterns or from pictures of famous structures, such as the Potala, the winter residence of the Dalai Lama, or Samye, the first monastery in Tibet. To obtain the deep reds, blues, and greens now found only in quality antique carpets from Tibet, he dyed the wool with vegetable dye made in Tibet or with RAM, an expensive dye imported from India. Because the wool was so fine, the carpets took longer to weave than they do now: a three-by-six-foot carpet took two people one month to produce, while they can now do it in 14 days.

Gyatso primarily wove saddle carpets on commission for landlords who owned horses. It was customary for the landlord to send a messenger with a gift of *chang*, or rice beer, to the house of the carpet master and to ask that the master come to the landlord's home to weave a carpet. While working on the project, the weaver, as were all tradesmen in Tibet, was served his meals in the employer's home.

A seemingly commonplace affair, the manner in which a worker received his food illustrated his status within the implicit hierarchy of tradesmen. The Tibetan proverb "Eat out, always go hungry; wear new clothes, always go cold" sheds light on this distinction. Tibetans are very conscious of the impression they make in public. Performing the correct behavior proves one's high status, a quality that is valued far more than an individual's temporary comfort or actual needs. The carpet master was served his rice, a rare and expensive treat, in a china bowl. If the landlord was serving meat, the carpet master received it in a woven basket. The weaver could eat as much food as he wanted but he could take none of it home with him. A spinner or a tailor was given his rice on a plate. He too could eat as much as he wanted but he had a choice: eat the food at the employer's house or take it home in a bag. This distinction implied that weavers, being of a higher status, did not need to take food with them because they provided well for their families. The spinners or tailors, on the other hand, were seen as being unable to make ends meet.

Since 1961, when Tibetans first began weaving carpets in exile, the craft has evolved into the largest handicraft industry in Nepal. Thousands of workers, Nepalese as well as Tibetan, are employed in the carpet factories. There is no longer an apprenticeship, and weavers are now able to learn the skill in a matter of months. Traditionally, the weaver was both an artist and a skilled worker; he designed and wove the carpets for which he earned his reputation. Weavers now follow designs plotted onto graph paper by carpet designers, whose jobs require more mathematical ability than artistic talent. And, because the work is seen mainly as a source of income, there is little emphasis on individual innovation by either designers or weavers.

In the early years in exile, according to Gyatso, the refugees had tried to weave carpets as they had in Tibet. The designs were typically Tibetan: dragons, phoenixes, lotus flowers, and other auspicious religious symbols woven in vibrant colors. To sell, however, the carpets had to appeal to the taste of the non-Tibetan buyers. Because the European market, where most of the carpets are sold, stressed muted tones woven in simple patterns surrounded by a basic border, these styles have almost completely replaced the more traditional carpets. Itan Mariz, the first European to import Tibetan carpets on a large scale, wanted thicker carpets rather than thin ones made from finer wool. To achieve the desired thickness, he convinced the weavers to switch to thicker rods which, from an expert's standpoint, resulted in a lower-quality carpet. Thicker wool is used now, and the Swiss-made Santose (Sandoz) dye does not create colors as brilliant as the RAM used previously. Finally, the faster a carpet is woven, the more profit it brings.

Thus carpet weaving is no longer an art in its own right. As with any art form that becomes an industry, compromises in quality must be made; carpets have become fashionable and are thus governed by the whims of fashion. Gyatso recognizes that carpet weaving is no longer a respected skill; it is now a common trade that can be picked up in a matter of days. He would only be interested in weaving a carpet of the quality he previously wove if he could get a good price for it.

* * * * *

On 10 December 1960, while walking down the dirt road leading to the refugee school in Jawalakhel, Father Moran passed what he described as a "gypsy-looking man" carrying several long boards. The gypsy explained that he was going to build a loom for weaving carpets. "It hit me," Father Moran said, "no one is making carpets in Nepal; all of the rugs are coming from India and Iran. Here is a new industry for Nepal where the Tibetans won't compete with the Nepalese at all!" He told the man, "Don't run away, Come with me. I'll find you a room and I will guarantee what you now make in one month you will make in one week. I will buy the wool, on one condition: you teach 10 refugees how to weave."

According to another account, Heidi Schultess, a professional Swiss weaver whose husband was a member of the Swiss mission in Kathmandu, introduced carpet weaving into the Tibetan community in Nepal. Shortly after arriving in Nepal, while wandering through the Kathmandu bazaar, Schultess discovered Ming Ma, a Tibetan carpet master weaving carpets with wool dyed in gaudy colors from Indian chemical dyes. She convinced him to return with her to Jawalakhel, where she helped him set up several looms in a small room attached to a building being enlarged by Tibetan carpenters under the supervision of Toni Hagen. Ming Ma's daughter and two other Tibetan women were recruited as weavers, and dozens of women were hired to spin the wool brought down from Tibet and the border areas of Nepal by Toni Hagen.

However the trade was in fact discovered, in early 1961 carpet weaving was introduced into the already existing crafts center in Jawalakhel. Under Ming Ma's direction, five looms were built, wool was purchased, and 20 young women were trained in weaving. Older Tibetans were put to work spinning the wool into balls and a local Nepalese was hired to teach teenage boys not interested in weaving how to wash and dye the wool.

Under the initial guidance of foreign aid workers and later under Tibetan management, traditional Tibetan carpet weaving slowly evolved from the small-scale craft of native Tibet into a handicraft industry which has not only been the backbone of the refugees' livelihood in Nepal, but has also become the second-largest earner of foreign currency in the entire country. The success of the carpet production far surpassed the expectations of even the most optimistic foreigners. Almost every Tibetan is involved in some aspect of the carpet industry; thus, in Nepal, being a producer of handwoven woolen carpets has become synonymous with being a Tibetan. In order to grasp their experience as refugees in Nepal, it is essential to understand the evolution and the nature of this industry.

The Tibetan government-in-exile estimates that of the approximately 20,000 refugees who passed into Nepal, 10,000 to 14,000 remained to settle there. The immediate and long-term needs of these Tibetans had to be addressed, and, because all of these tasks required a substantial amount of funding, money had to be raised. After a rather slow beginning, by 1963 assisting Tibetans had become quite popular and the aid program in Nepal had grown to "enormous, complex and costly proportions" (Joshi 1983:12). Because these foreigners were in large part responsible for the creation of the carpet industry, it is important to look at the transformations in the use of foreign aid before turning directly to that industry.

In 1963, ICRC was bearing the organizational responsibility for the entire project; in turn, it received financial, technical, and other assistance from a diverse collection of donors. Through its subsidiary office, the Swiss Association for Technical Assistance (SATA), the Service for Technical Cooperation of the Swiss government provided money and technical advisors for the four settlements in operation at this time: Tashi Palkhiel, on the outskirts of Pokhara; Jawalakhel, near Kathmandu; Dhorpatan, in the mountains of western Nepal; and Chialsa, in the foothills of Mount Everest. Since SATA's field office was located in Jawalakhel, the Swiss staff had daily contact with the refugee community; they distributed rations, provided health care, and, with Father Moran's committee, opened day schools in the first four settlements established.

From 1961 to 1963, the UNHCR also offered financial assistance to the ICRC. In September 1964, UNHCR opened an office in Kathmandu to deal specifically with the Tibetan situation. Initially this office was not very active; it was rumored that its first director preferred to conduct business from his swimming pool and the second one was more interested in trading antiques than in helping refugees. (In the late 1960s, when a more dedicated representative was appointed, UNHCR's assistance became more effective.) In 1965, this office was put in charge of settling those refugees who had not been included in the four original settlement camps. When the representative closed the organization's office in Nepal, UNHCR continued its involvement through the slowly expanding Nepal Red Cross.

US AID maintained a steady flow of food supplies to be distributed as free rations during the first few years. Other organizations, including the Australian Refugee Committee and the Swiss Red Cross, provided surplus milk powder, clothing, and medicine. The Dooley Foundation in the United States sent volunteers to train mothers in the day care center, and the Norwegian Refugee Council provided funds for building houses.

With so many organizations involved, confusion arose over who was responsible for various projects, and some things were neglected as a result. The entire project needed to be overseen and supervised by one group. ICRC, whose responsibility was to provide assistance to those in immediate need, had been fulfilling this role up until 1963, when the critical period for the refugees was over. Since SATA was the only other large organization involved on a grass-roots level, the government of Nepal asked the Swiss government to orchestrate the international assistance and to administer the four original settlements. On 22 November 1964, the Nepalese and Swiss governments concluded a written agreement officially documenting the role of the Swiss, which stated, "The spirit of cooperation in this agreement between the two governments aimed at making the Tibetans economically self-sufficient and at integrating them into Nepal."

That same year the land on which the four settlements had been built was legally purchased by His Majesty's Government of Nepal with money donated by UNHCR. Because only Nepalese citizens can own land, the settlement lands were registered under the name of the Nepal Red Cross, which in addition took on the responsibility of serving as trustee for the refugees. The organization was to assist the Tibetans in dealing with the Nepalese government and to represent their rights and interests whenever necessary.

The Swiss had acted with the understanding that after approximately a decade in exile, the Tibetans would be offered Nepalese citizenship and thus would be able to assume title to the land. By 1987, however, only a handful of refugees had become citizens and this tacit land agreement was still in effect. Although there is no legal document explaining the arrangement, the present head of the Nepal Red Cross stated that this organization will never tax the Tibetans for the land nor will it ever back down on its responsibility as outlined in the agreement.

When the Swiss inherited the responsibility for the four settlements in 1964, the Jawalakhel craft center where Karma's mother was working

Families live in two or three rooms in the brick complex built in Jawalakhel with foreign assistance in 1965. Privacy is limited and sanitation facilities in constant disrepair; many families have chosen to move out of the settlement into nearby rooms rented from Nepalese. ©Peter Forbes

specialized in carpet weaving, sweater knitting, and belt weaving. Of these handicrafts, the carpet work involved the greatest numbers of refugees, held the greatest potential for expansion, and did not conflict with any fundamental Tibetan values. This craft drew on skills that were familiar to the Tibetans, and it offered opportunities for more the assertive members of the community to exercise the entrepreneurial skills for which they are now famous. The Swiss thus chose to focus exclusively on establishing this craft as the economic foundation for the refugees.

A permanent brick weaving hall was constructed on land across from the refugees' grass huts. In 1965, the Australian Refugee Committee and UNHCR donated funds to replace the bamboo shacks with the brick-and-mud houses in which the refugees still live today. At the same time, the Swiss began to tackle the first major task: recruiting and maintaining a steady work force that would consistently produce high-quality goods. Regardless of how hard they worked or whether they worked at all, during the first few years in Jawalakhel the entire community had been receiving daily food rations free of charge. Soon some began to expect food without having to work much; they saw no reason why they should now work all day in an unfamiliar, unappealing job when they could eat for free.

In the early 1960s, before SATA took responsibility for the crafts center, foreigners in charge of the camp had temporarily stopped food rations in Jawalakhel to force the weavers to start working. When the rations were reinstituted, the factory workers were told to choose whether they wanted to get paid in food or in money. Even with these changes, however, the weavers remained in the center only a few hours each day; the carpets were often so carelessly and sloppily woven that they could never be sold. A Tibetan assistant for ICRC and later for SATA remembered: "The men especially did not like working in the factories. Spinning and carding wool was the women's work and in Tibet men would never touch women's work." He continued, "Both the men and women were very lazy. In Tibet, this wasn't their job. There they would go out to look after the cattle and yak all day and then come home, eat, and go to sleep. In the beginning they felt very sorry for themselves." The Swiss interpreted the Tibetans' unwillingness to work a bit differently:

> The Tibetans were skilled but they lacked the enthusiasm for work. They wanted to take full advantage of their status as refugees and live on charity and surplus food provided by US AID. They retained this attitude for many years, partly as they lacked education and did not value the self-respect which comes from supporting oneself and partly due to uncertainty as to whether they might not soon return to Tibet. The great problem for SATA was to create in their minds the concept that those who could work should do so. (Joshi 1983:10)

Finally, in an attempt to increase the quality of the carpets produced and the speed with which they were woven, in 1965 the Swiss switched from a daily wage to one based on the actual amount of work completed. As the Tibetans realized that the size of their salary correlated directly with the amount they wove, the Swiss's problem was solved. The challenge now came in finding a market for the accumulating piles of carpets.

In his haste to leave Tibet in 1959, the Dalai Lama had not brought along any of the treasures of the Potala. Luckily, however, on an earlier journey to Sikkim, he had brought 1,000 pack animals—each one carrying 120 pounds of gold, silver, and ancient coins later valued at $987,500 (Avedon 1984:91). A significant portion of this treasure was used to provide capital for the refugee settlements first established in India and Nepal; it was also added to money from SATA, ICRC, UNHCR, and the Tibetan community itself to finance the first carpet centers. An ongoing market for the carpets had to be found, however.

Because Jawalakhel is near Kathmandu, which since the 1950s has had a steadily increasing foreign population, some carpets could be sold locally.

In 1961, just after the crafts center was established, Monique Anderson, who was assisting Heidi Schultess with the carpet weavers, organized a carpet show at AID to display the Tibetan handicrafts made in the Jawalakhel center and to raise money for the refugees. An alley of prayer flags leading to the exposition was erected and wooden looms where the Tibetans could demonstrate their work were set up. Wealthy refugees lent silver bowls, turquoise jewelry, and ancient silk thankhas to decorate the room. The show was a tremendous success, and generated enough orders to keep the center busy for the next six months.

A small carpet shop was also set up in the Royal Hotel. Gradually, as the word spread, foreigners began to seek out the factory to buy carpets. Father Moran contacted Sears and Roebuck, which agreed to buy 1,000 identical carpets—but only if they were identical. Since part of the attraction of the handwoven carpets was that each one was unique, Father Moran looked elsewhere for buyers.

By the time SATA assumed responsibility for the handicraft center, a tremendous number of unsold carpets had piled up. The Swiss at first dismissed the idea of exporting carpets to Europe; at wholesale prices, the carpets would generate less money than local sales, and, more important, the refugees knew absolutely nothing about exporting or foreign trade. Without some way of generating an income, however, the future of the entire resettlement program would be jeopardized and the Swiss's investment would be wasted. So, despite their reluctance, they began to investigate the overseas market.

In 1966, the Swiss established a carpet trading company as a separate entity from the three SATA handicraft centers that were operating in Jawalakhel, Chialsa, and Tashi Palkhiel. The company was to supply the three centers with raw materials, keep the designers up to date on the design trends of the market, and promote the carpets in foreign countries. The profit generated from carpet sales was to be put toward needy causes in the four existing settlements. The company, which was jointly owned by the Dalai Lama, the Swiss government and the Tibetan community, was registered on 1 January 1969 as the Tibetan Carpet Trading Company. This name soon created a misunderstanding between the Nepalese and Chinese governments. Nepalese ministers requested that the Swiss delete the word *Tibetan*; in return, they promised to give the company import/export exemption status. The word was cut but the tax exemption was never granted. Now called the Carpet Trading Company (CTC), the offices are located in the three-story, whitewashed, stone Rana Palace in Jawalakhel that was first used as a health clinic for the refugees and was purchased by SATA in the early 1960s.

Shortly thereafter, the Swiss manager of CTC organized a carpet show in Switzerland to introduce the products to the European market. There he met the German carpet importer Itan Mariz, who expressed interest in buying all of the export-quality carpets CTC had in stock and in regularly purchasing as many carpets as the SATA handicraft centers could produce. This greatly eased the financial burden on SATA and the other aid organizations, and represented a major hurdle in the transition of carpet weaving into a large-scale industry.

*   *   *   *   *

From the very beginning the Swiss planned for their presence to be temporary; their primary objective was to make the settlements into self-supporting units. Thus SATA did not only focus on the carpet centers, but also invested in schools, in cooperatives where the refugees could buy commodities at lower prices, and in health clinics. However, there also had to be a cadre of Tibetans with the ability and the interest to manage these structures efficiently and effectively. According to a SATA report, "It doesn't seem that qualified Tibetan personnel are at present available in the centers in Nepal, as most of the people who showed greater ability and initiative have left for India" (SATA 1965:2). Young men migrated to India to join the army, families moved so that their children could attend the Tibetan schools in India, and many headed south simply to be closer to the Dalai Lama. This left young children, old people, or those too sick to travel while the border was still open.

In an effort to address this scarcity, SATA organized administrative and teacher training programs for refugees from all of the SATA camps. Using a placement test, the Swiss selected 22 young Tibetan men and women from the camps in Chialsa, Jawalakhel, Tashi Palkhiel, and Dhorpatan for the second three-year administrative course. Karma, the child who had traveled from western Tibet to Jawalakhel with his parents (see Chapter 2), now a young man of 20, was selected to participate in the program. Karma was one of the first students to go to the handicraft centers; he was selected to work in a small umbrella organization created by the Swiss to oversee the welfare needs of all of the refugees in the four camps. Other students were offered positions as settlement managers, accountants, or assistants at CTC. Even with this pool of trained applicants, however, many of the positions in Nepal still had to be filled with government-in-exile staff transferred from India.

In 1986, only five of the twenty-two trained in the second program were still working for the Tibetan government-in-exile, and young people who had participated in other training programs offered in the remote camps have since moved to Kathmandu. A member of the Swiss staff working in Chialsa in 1970 comments on this migration:

> We really gave them good facilities for training—whatever we could give we would. And that made them leave Chialsa. We thought in giving them training they could then really run the settlement—but Kathmandu was always the big attraction. And when the young ones left, eventually the parents would also.

The training courses were given to enable Tibetans to run their own communities, but leadership positions are usually low paying and located in remote camps, several days' walk from Kathmandu. Confronted with these prospects, the responsibility of serving the Tibetan community has not been enough to motivate many of these students to continue working for the government-in-exile.

*　　　*　　　*　　　*　　　*

In 1966 the handicraft centers in Jawalakhel, Chialsa, and Tashi Palkhiel were converted into private limited partnerships managed by those Tibetans who had served as assistants to the Swiss staff. Some Swiss personnel stayed on for several more years as technical advisors to ensure the smooth transfer of responsibilities. At this time effective management included producing export-quality carpets, administering the small day schools previously run by Father Moran's committee, providing health care, and overseeing the general needs of the community. The newly trained staff was overwhelmed. Although the company was able to bear some of the economic burdens on the handicraft center staff, too often the welfare needs of the communities were inadequately met.

Thus on 25 February 1972, Dr. Hogger, the head of SATA, founded the Snow Lion Foundation. The foundation was created as an umbrella organization to procure funds and oversee projects involving the health, education, and social welfare of those Tibetan settlements managed by SATA. Dr. Hogger expressed his confidence that the foundation would bring "further solidarity among the Tibetans in Nepal...and as a legal body [it] would give confidence to possible donors" (Hogger 1972).

Dr. Hogger deposited 20,000 rupees in a bank as fixed capital to start the foundation. It was to meet its running expenses with the combination of the interest from this capital, grants from the three handicraft centers and CTC, and donations from international organizations. Today, 50 percent of the foundation's funds go toward education: to pay teacher salaries, buy books, repair school buildings, and provide scholarship money. The foundation also supplies the elderly and the handicapped with small stipends, looks after the basic health needs of the camp inhabitants, and assists in the one-time construction and reconstruction needs of settlement buildings. Because the Snow Lion Foundation depends on the handicraft center for much of its income, its financial stability fluctuates with the economics of the carpet industry. The increasing price of wool and the greater competition from new factories are eating away at the centers' profits and thus at the foundation's income. More and more, the secretary of the Snow Lion Foundation is being forced to seek new funding sources in order to keep the foundation solvent.

Although for the most part successful, the Swiss's work in the Tibetan communities was not without its share of complications and misunderstandings—some minor and some more serious—as Tibetan and Swiss values clashed. A rather telling example of such a disagreement is the Tibetans' slow response to letters. On 6 November 1974, Dr. E. Weiderkehr of Swiss Aid to Tibetans wrote to the Dalai Lama's representative in Nepal: "I was surprised to hear that my letter of August 15 had safely arrived. And you did not even take the trouble to reply to it. Your office is not very efficient I must say" (Weiderkehr 1974). The members of the government-in-exile office, it should be pointed out, had probably seen their first typewriter only several years earlier, and did not yet understand the Swiss value of punctuality—nor how, by accommodating it, they could more easily gain what they wanted.

In another instance a carpet with "Om Mani Padme Hum" woven within a colorful border was made for export. After this carpet was sent to Europe, rumors that the carpet would be used on the floor where these sacred letters would be walked upon spread rapidly through the Tibetan community. The weavers angrily reproached the Tibetan welfare officer for exchanging the sanctity of Tibetan culture for the profit of a carpet sale. In contrast to other issues on which the refugees were slow to respond, this question, which was of utmost importance to the entire Tibetan community, was solved by the Tibetans and foreigners within three weeks. Tags were added to the carpets that explained the religious significance of the characters and emphasized that these carpets were to be used exclusively as wall decorations.

The Swiss attempt to create a poultry farm at the center in Jawalakhel created more serious conflicts. The poultry farm was introduced to provide younger refugees with an alternative to the carpet factory. In the late 1960s, before Karma was chosen for the administrative course, the manager of the Jawalakhel factory asked him to leave his weaving job and enter a poultry training program. Karma, however, quickly discovered his preference for weaving. He recalls:

> I didn't like the poultry job, not because the work was dirty but because it

kills so many insects. Millions of insects die, and after six weeks the boiler was ready to be killed for meat and after 18 months when the chickens could not lay enough eggs, they were sold for meat. So, its all killing, killing, killing.

The poultry farm never really got off the ground, and it was closed after four years. The Swiss attributed this failure to "negligence and lack of proper management from the Tibetan side after the Swiss supervisors left" (Joshi 1983:15). Although the poultry farm did fail in part because of the refugees' lack of expertise, from the Tibetan point of view, the project was not successful because "killing chickens was a sin to the people and they never really approved of the endeavor" (Joshi 1983:15).

Similar misunderstandings occurred in each of the camps. At one point in Jawalakhel, relations between the Swiss and the refugees became so tense that an officer was flown in from Geneva to make staff changes in SATA's field office. Gradually, through trial and error, the Swiss realized that projects in which the Tibetans had no financial stake were probably going to fail. "The Tibetans will take an interest in a scheme only if their own money is involved in it. Otherwise, if the scheme fails, foreign money only will be lost" (Weiderkehr n.d.). For the most part, however, the Swiss and the Tibetans were on surprisingly good terms. The problems that did arise simply served as a reminder to the Swiss that the aim of their work was not to support the refugee community indefinitely. Their objective was to help the refugees become self-supporting and to integrate them into Nepalese society as quickly as possible.

Even into the early 1970s, however, the Swiss were still entrenched in almost every aspect of the refugees' lives. In 1970, Annie Gundali and her husband, both employees of SATA, were responsible for overseeing the Chialsa handicraft center, running the settlement school and dispensary, constructing new houses, roofing old leaky buildings, and organizing community meetings. She created a school garden where the students could learn how to grow vegetables to sell at the local bazaar. Teachers came to her room in the morning for guidance in their lesson planning. Old and handicapped refugees who had no relatives and monks and nuns with no other means of support still received food rations from the Swiss. Gundali gradually cut back these rations because he wanted the Tibetans to realize it was the community's responsibility to look after its own needy. Even so, Ms. Gundali stated that "as long as the refugees could get sources from elsewhere, they would rather ask for help." She continued, "I think we created that among the Tibetans, we were really taking care of them for too long a time, too long giving them things to eat, distributing things. They got used to the system of asking for help." Mr. Rana, a SATA employee in Dhorpatan, recalls, "How many years can you give aid? That was a problem for us. Our duty was to make them self-sufficient but the Tibetan habit is such that if you give to them they will always say, give us more. How to ease out?"

The Swiss tried to remove themselves from Dhorpatan as diplomatically as possible. The Tibetans there were able to live off the potatoes they were growing. Mr. Rana told the refugees that SATA would repair the roofs of leaky houses and that he would work to solve recurring problems with locals over grazing land. When these tasks were accomplished, the Swiss would leave. In Tashi Palkhiel, on the other hand, there was no farm land and the handicraft center was running with only 10 to 12 weavers. Some refugees managed to get jobs as laborers on the road being built around Pokhara after the Swiss stopped providing assistance; the majority, however, were unable to make a living, and many moved to Kathmandu where life, they heard, was easier.

The Swiss had assured the Tibetans that they "would not withdraw without leaving behind a structure on which the refugees could rely." When the last Swiss advisor left in 1972, SATA had fulfilled this promise. The refugees in the SATA camps now had the economic foundation on which to build their communities. The most significant contribution SATA made to ensuring the future success of the Tibetan communities in Nepal, however, seems to have been identifying and developing a product that could be competitive on an international market. After making the initial contacts, the Swiss left the direction of the carpet industry up to the Tibetans. And, having taken far greater advantage of this opportunity than the Swiss ever envisioned, the Tibetans are now active participants in Nepalese and the international economy. Most important, they are providing opportunities for their children to enter an industry that has evolved into a uniquely Tibetan enterprise.

Chapter 5

Himalayan Exporters

Approximately 2,000 Tibetans were living in the Kathmandu valley in 1965. The Jawalakhel settlement, which housed 700 refugees, was at full capacity. Most of the remaining Tibetans gravitated to the stupas at Boudha and Swayambhunath. These sites had no formal settlements, so the refugees stayed in Nepali houses or in tents set up in the rice fields. Health care was irregular, food rations were sporadic, and schools were nonexistent. Middle-aged Tibetans hawked their jewels, and elders huddled near the stupa, begging for food. The children were malnourished and the teenagers were troublemakers. One advantage of living so close to the stupas was that the Tibetans could have daily contact with their spiritual leaders who gathered there. These Tibetans were willing to forgo steady rations and job security for the sense of continuity and stability gained from being close to two of their holiest temples.

In 1971 Gyalo Thondup, the Dalai Lama's second-eldest brother, visited Nepal. He was shocked at the condition of the refugees living five miles away from Jawalakhel, in Boudha. Upon his return to India, he immediately set out to create some form of employment for this group. Providing the initial financing from his personal funds, Gyalo convinced the previous manager of the Jawalakhel handicraft center, who had left government service to pursue private business, to set up the factory along with four Tibetans from India.

Wangchuck Tsering owns a private carpet factory in Boudha, a restaurant and a guest house in the tourist section of Kathmandu, and a clothing store managed by his wife on Kanti Path. Tall and aristocratic-looking, he lives in a well-furnished home in Thamel. When he and his uncle left Tibet on a trip to India to honor the Buddha's birthday in 1956, the Chinese invasion prevented them from returning home. Since he had received formal schooling in Tibet and could speak some English and Hindi, Wangchuck Tsering was called upon by Tibetan leaders to translate articles in Indian papers for the newspaper *Tibet Freedom*. Several years later he was transferred to Delhi to work in the branch office of the government-in-exile. "There were so many difficulties at that time," he recalls. "There were shortages of everything and there were not enough people, but it was exciting; I was young and I enjoyed the work very much." In 1965 he and seven other Tibetans were chosen to enter a training program in community development at Cornell University in Ithaca, New York. After two years in the United States, he reported back to Dharmsala and was immediately sent to Boudha by Gyalo Thondup.

Unlike the refugees in the Swiss camps, the managers in Boudha had no financial assistance, no technical advisors, no international connections, and no administrative training courses. "It was quite a challenge," Wangchuck recalls. "At first I had no experience in business. Suddenly I had to make one rupee become two rupees. It was really a very big change for me." They did, however, have the SATA model and their own fierce loyalties to the Tibetan cause to fall back on.

Like the Swiss in Jawalakhel, these Tibetans first had to find employeees for their factory. Wangchuck walked along the stone pathway encircling the stupa and explained to the refugees begging there that he had been sent by the government in Dharmsala to help them. They were opening a carpet factory, he said; jobs, permanent accommodations for employees, allowances for the elderly, and an education for their children were all available. At first only seven weavers came to work; then 12 came, then 13 and 14. After a year or so, finding weavers was no longer a problem; marketing the finished product, however, was.

Initially called Gelek and Company after one of the founding members, the handicraft center was soon divided into Boudha Handicraft (BHC), which was to look after production of carpets, and Himalayan Carpet Exporters (HCE), managed by Wangchuck Tsering, which was to market the finished product. By 1973 the factory employed 60 workers, 40 of whom wove carpets, and all of whom required a salary. Lots of carpets were being produced, but very little capital. The managers could not cut back on production because providing the workers with employment and a salary was the sole reason for the factory's existence. Gyalo Thondup could not afford to assume the financial burden for the factory's future. Because the companies had no access to outside organizations to provide temporary support, their survival depended on a market.

On New Road, one of Kathmandu's main thoroughfares, HCE opened a small craft shop managed by Wangchuck Tsering's wife. At a carpet display set up along the dirt road leading to the stupa in Boudha, workers explained to passing tourists the Tibetans' plight. Wangchuck Tsering asked travel agencies to add the center to the tourist bus route. A few sales were made through these endeavors, but they were not nearly enough. The Swiss, when faced with the same dilemma, had looked to the export market in Europe; the Tibetans at HCE, however, had no such foreign contacts. Wangchuck was responsible for selling the carpets, yet he was forbidden to travel overseas without a Nepalese passport. (Tibetans in India, on the other hand, can travel internationally with their refugee identity cards.)

One day a German carpet importer happened to visit the stupa. Interested in the carpets and moved by the tale of Tibet and its refugees, he ordered one shipment of carpets, and then another, and then another. This albeit inconsistent market alleviated the crisis significantly, yet the center still searched for a larger and more stable client. Desperately, Wangchuck wrote letters to possible buyers in Europe. In 1974, Mr. Haffner, the owner of a European carpet importing company, Oriental Carpet Manufacturers (OCM), began importing HCE's export-quality stock. Because OCM's demand for carpets was far greater than the Boudha factory could produce, HCE used both the capital generated by selling the carpets from the Boudha factory and the now-guaranteed market of OCM to assist fledgling Tibetan carpet centers around the country. The arrangement worked well for both sides, and eventually an agreement was reached that OCM would be HCE's only customer.

Today, to protect OCM's carpet designs, outsiders cannot enter the center in Boudha without permission and they are forbidden from taking photographs. HCE's exports have grown from 1,500 square meters in 1974 to 11,000 square meters in 1979. The company now finances, produces, and exports the carpets for six weaving centers in Nepal, three in Pokhara, two in Kathmandu, and a small one north of Pokhara, in Tserok. HCE is bigger than the Carpet Trading Company factories that were started with foreign assistance, and it is the second-largest carpet exporting company in Nepal.

On the western side of Kathmandu, near Swayambhunath, Tibetans joined together to organize celebrations of Tibetan festivals and to work with the Tibetan welfare officer to to ensure that the refugees obeyed the laws of the land. Their activities were financed with donations from wealthier Tibetans and a small spinning and weaving factory was set up in Swayambhunath. This center survived on its own until the mid-1970s, when HCE assumed responsibility for the finances and marketing of the center.

*   *   *   *   *

In 1963 a group of nomads from Saka district in western Tibet trickled down to Pokhara from the northern border of Nepal. Having worn out their welcome in the north, they set up their tents in a grassy field near the Pokhara airstrip. At first they lived off the free rations flown into Pokhara by ICRC. A few built grass huts and a number sought out temporary jobs breaking stones for the road under construction from Kathmandu. After two years, His Majesty's Government of Nepal declared that the refugees had to relocate, and offered them a remarkably low price for an empty stretch of land called *Tsore Patan* ("abandoned area"), five km to the south.

The land had been abandoned because of the numerous deaths that had occurred there, leading the Nepalese to believe it was haunted. Unable to refuse the price, UNHCR, instructed by ICRC to assist the refugees coming into Pokhara, bought the land and established a temporary settlement for the refugees. Because of the impermanence of the settlement, and also probably because of administrative problems at UNHCR, no employment opportunities were created for the refugees. ICRC and Father Moran's committee had their hands full elsewhere, and although some of the Tibetans living in the settlement called Tashi Ling continued to work at road construction sites, the majority simply begged and waited for food rations to arrive.

A crafts center where woolen cloth was woven for local sale was finally opened by the Nepal Red Cross with funds from UNHCR in 1966. Tailoring and woodworking projects were also initiated by the Red Cross, but neither lasted. In 1967, the Norwegian Refugee Council started a pig and poultry farm but the Tibetans quickly lost interest. Under the Norwegians' guidance, the refugees cultivated 12 acres of land with maize, groundnut, wheat, and potatoes. Only the potatoes grew; the rest failed because the soil was dry and stony, and any crops that did begin to grow were quickly eaten by wild animals. In the mid-1970's, the Nepal Red Cross copied the SATA camps' idea and introduced carpet weaving into the small crafts center which at that time employed 42 workers. However, the organization had no capital, no foreign contacts, and little experience in managing an industry. Because it could not establish any foreign markets, the factory had to depend on sporadic sales to the random tourists who traveled all the way to Pokhara. Tibetans sent to Tashi Ling by the Tibetan government-in-exile in India to work with the Nepalese instead simply quarreled with their counterparts, and the factory was plagued with rumors of corruption and dishonesty. "There were so many problems," Wangchuck Tsering said. "Those who could leave the camp left for Kathmandu so those that remained behind were in a very pitiful condition."

For several years Wangchuck Tsering tried to convince the Nepal Red Cross to transfer the management to of the factory to HCE. The exporting company could provide raw wool for weaving, a market for the carpets, money for the weaver's salaries, and advice from its experience in Boudha. Wangchuck assured the Nepalese that the Tibetans at HCE would be more responsible than their Tibetan predecessors, that the Nepal Red Cross would not have to worry about losing its investment. The director of the Nepal Red Cross finally decided to give the Tibetans another opportunity, and in 1980 it sold 49 percent of the company to HCE and handed over the management to Wangchuck.

Mr. Sandup, a thin, energetic man educated in India, was transferred from his teaching position in Jawalakhel in 1980 to rejuvenate the notoriously poor and difficult settlement. Prospects in Tashi Ling when he arrived were not very encouraging: the settlers were rude and quarrelsome, complaining about the assignment of carpets to weave and fighting over the occasional foreign aid. They refused to help the poorer members of the community and expressed no interest in cooperating with the new manager. Their stone houses were dilapidated, sanitation facilities pitiful, and everyone was dirty and unkempt. "It was very, very difficult in the beginning," Mr. Sandup recalls. "The people were very spoiled."

Under the Nepal Red Cross, the workers had received daily wages; they would casually wander over to the small, stone weaving hall where they would sign their names, collect their five-rupee salaries, and return home. Production was inconsistent: sometimes all the weavers were needed, other times only half were called on, and often the whole factory was closed. When Mr. Sandup announced that the weavers would be paid only for the amount of work completed, most of the refugees simply refused to work. Those who did go stood waiting by the factory at eight o'clock idly chatting with their neighbors, but would not begin work until the bell rang at nine. The weavers then wove for a few hours and returned home. Eventually, as in other factories, as a few hard workers began to make money others realized that they, too, could earn something, and production gradually increased.

Today the factory is in full swing. Work is constant and people speak highly of the new manager and the progress that has been made. Mr. Sandup also speaks favorably of the changes in the refugees' attitudes, of their increased willingness to work toward improving the quality of life in the settlement, and of their cooperation. He finds a sense of community among Tibetans in the Pokhara area — where most refugees continue to live in one of the four government-in-exile settlements — that he had found lacking in Kathmandu, where many Tibetans are living and working on their own.

* * * * *

Introduced by the Swiss as a way of assisting the small number of refugees with whom they were involved, the carpet weaving industry was quickly adopted by Tibetan leaders as a way of establishing a secure economic base for all of the refugees in Nepal. Unlike in India, where the refugees are involved in a wide range of enterprises, by the early 1980s carpet weaving had evolved into the primary source of income for the entire Tibetan community in Nepal. The lucrativeness of this industry and thus the increasing affluence of the refugees is similarly unique among the refugees in Nepal. The Tibetans in Nepal are increasingly associated with this wealth by refugees living elsewhere, who interpret this success as both a source for cultural preservation and a cause for cultural dissipation.

Chapter 6

Horse Traders and Entrepreneurs

> We say we must work double time than Nepalese. The Nepalese have everything—this is their country, it is where they were born. They have their heritage, their grandfather's money and property from generations ago. We have to pay for everything, rent for a house, food, water, electricity. We have nothing; everything was taken by the Chinese.
> —*Ugen Tsering, owner of Utse's Restaurant, Thamel*

Shortly after the sound of pounding hammers announces the beginning of the work day in the Jawalakhel factory, private shop owners leave home to open their carpet shops. Although a growing number of those with private shops continue to live in the settlement, the majority live on their own in rooms rented from local Nepalese. Dechen, a 20-year-old who dropped out of a Tibetan school in India at 18, looks after her family store. After unlocking the heavy lock to guard against the increasing number of break-ins, she sweeps the floor, hangs carpets on the door for display, and sits down to gossip with her neighbors. Farther up the street the wife of the handicraft center's manager arrives with her two-year-old son to open their shop; across the road a fifteen-year-old boy sweeps out the store where he works. Depending on the number of tourists—the main source of business—the hours slip by with gossip, card games, gambling, and people-watching. Groups form and disperse; games begin and end; news quickly spreads, and occasionally a carpet is sold. At five o'clock, before the hammers cease their pounding, the doors are closed and locked

An increasing number of refugees are choosing to open their own carpet shops where they sell their goods to tourists visiting Nepal. ©Peter Forbes

and the shopkeepers head home to prepare dinner.

Not all Tibetans in the Kathmandu valley were suited for, or interested in, working for the carpet factories. Some disliked the work, others preferred to work for themselves. Unlike India, where many Indians were already well established in business, Tibetans arrived in Nepal just as the country's economy was beginning to develop; businesspeople came across few regulations and fewer competitors. Travelers had just begun to discover Nepal and the tourist market left plenty of room for expansion. Business opportunities existed for those refugees willing to take advantage of them.

In 1968, Ugen Tsering came to Nepal on vacation from his home in a refugee camp in India. He was unhappy in India. "Camps are for families," he said. "If you have a wife and children it's good to settle down in a camp. I was a bachelor, I did not want to settle." He decided to try his luck in Nepal, where he had a few friends for whom he could work and where he could live independently. When Himalayan Carpet Exporters opened a curio shop in Kathmandu to sell jackets, carpets, and other handicraft items, he got a job working in the showroom five hours a day. Before and after work, Ugen climbed onto his black one-speed bicycle and visited tourists he had met in the shop at their hotels to try to sell them Tibetan handicrafts borrowed from his wealthier friends. The HCE shop did very little business—perhaps because one of its employees was competing against it—and it was soon closed. Wangchuck Tsering offered Ugen a job at the center in Boudha, but Ugen declined because the salary was too low, explaining, "I have to earn my extra money in the morning and at night and I have to do it in Kathmandu because that is where the tourists are. Boudha is too far away." After leaving the job, Ugen roamed around doing odd jobs, and then, with a friend who was a cook, decided to open a small restaurant in Thamel.

After spending two years as a trekking guide for US Vietnam vets and AID workers, Pu Kelsang took a job as a carpet designer for the Carpet Trading Company because, he said, he had been exceptionally good at drawing in school. While he was employed by CTC, his wife began weaving carpets in their home at night after she returned from her job in the factory at Jawalakhel. After work, Pu took these carpets down to Durbar Marg and rolled them out on the sidewalk in front of the Annapurna Hotel, one of the most expensive hotels in the country. He was quite successful at selling, not necessarily because of the quality of the product, but rather because tourists were intrigued by the tragic story of Tibet and wanted to help. After a few years at CTC, Pu had a disagreement with the Swiss over the large discrepancy between his salary and that of the Swiss carpet designer; and he quit.* He then concentrated entirely on selling his own carpets.

In 1961 the Tibetan government-in-exile sent Mr. Thinley to work in Jawalakhel as a translator, teaching the English alphabet to the children in the settlement school and helping to organize and manage the cooperative. After several years he was transferred to the Tibetan camp in Darjeeling, in the hills of eastern India. By this time, however, Thinley had a wife who was half Nepalese and several young children. He told the government-in-exile that if he could help the Tibetans in Jawalakhel he would continue to work for them, but that he would not move. When his transfer was not rescinded, he quit.

His wife was weaving carpets at home, so he set up several more looms and hired weavers from the camp factory to come weave until eleven o'clock at night. He bought the wool locally and paid to have it dyed at the handicraft center. Thinley also began collecting old Tibetan carpets and other antiques carried into exile by some of the wealthier Tibetans. At first, he invited Westerners, mostly Americans, to his house to look at his

---

* It is common in aid organizations for foreigners' salaries to be on the scale of their country, while the salaries of host country employees are on the scale of the host country.

carpets. Shortly thereafter, in a small bamboo hut near the big tree that marks the center of the Tibetan area in Jawalakhel, he opened the first private Tibetan shop, selling old handicrafts from Tibet and newly woven carpets. Over the years, this first makeshift store has been replaced, and the large tree is now surrounded by 50 or more single-room, cement-floored carpet shops.

In 1971 Ugen Tsering and his friend the cook opened their restaurant, Utse's, in Thamel, a neighborhood which at that time was so dangerous that even rickshaw drivers refused to go there at night. Other Tibetans thought they were crazy and predicted that the enterprise would quickly fail. A few months later, about the time the restaurant had been doomed to go under, the Peace Corps opened a training center around the corner that housed 30 or 40 Peace Corps volunteers. As soon as one group finished its three-month course, another immediately replaced it. The volunteers ate breakfast and dinner at the center, but for lunch they were free to go wherever they wished. Since the choices were limited, they quickly discovered Utse's, and business boomed.

Since then, Ugen's enterprise has been a tremendous success. Every morning he bicycles to the local markets to buy his own vegetables so he can maintain the quality of his food. He now has 17 Nepalese on staff; he rarely hires Tibetans because, he says, "Tibetans don't want to work for somebody else. They want to do their own things." Eventually Thamel was cleaned up; situated in the northwestern section of downtown Kathmandu, it is now the bustling center for low- to medium-budget tourists, world travelers, and trekkers. Tiny, one-room shops overflowing with cheap cotton clothing, antiques, backpacking equipment, and books line the streets. Restaurants crowded between and above the stores advertise apple pie, brownies, whole wheat bread, and fruit museli on big colorful signs.

Tired of carrying his merchandise around on his back as he pedaled a bicycle, Pu Kelsang decided to open a carpet shop on Durbar Marg with capital acquired from selling a piece of land his family had owned for generations in Solu Khumbu. Durbar Marg, the main drag leading through Kathmandu to the king's palace, is lined with hotels, restaurants, and shops that cater to the wealthier tourists, offering higher quality and more expensive services than those found elsewhere in Nepal. His store, the first of its kind on this street, was an immediate success. A few years later he bought land in Jawalakhel and opened the first private carpet factory in Nepal. He hired Nepalese weavers—not a conscious decision, he says, but simply because most Tibetans were busy and did not want to work outside the government-in-exile factory or for another Tibetan. Another Tibetan remarked that some people saw his move as a betrayal of the Tibetan cause. By employing Nepalese, he was taking the art out of the Tibetans' hands; by opening a private export company that would compete with the government-in-exile centers, he was undermining the economic security of the Tibetan community.

Nevertheless, Pu set about establishing what is now the largest carpet exporting factory in Nepal. In 1986, he employed 2,000 workers and exported 2,000–3,000 square meters per month. (In comparison, CTC, the third-largest exporting factory in Nepal, exports 1,500 square meters per month.) Pu owns a four-story house, four cars, and two video machines, and travels regularly to Europe on business.

A soft-spoken, polite man, Pu is humble and rather guarded when discussing his remarkable success. It is rumored, however, that he is a difficult person to work for, that he is domineering and manipulative and will go to whatever lengths necessary to make a profit. It is also said that he prays fervently every morning and that he contributes large sums of money to monasteries in the Kathmandu valley. He owns a house in Solu Khumbu that needs repair, yet he has not been back there for 15 years because he is too busy. "If the plane couldn't fly and bring me back to Kathmandu (which it often can't do), work would pile up too much." He cannot remember much about conditions in the camps in the 1960s because he says, "Mostly I was working . . . I know only my business, nothing else."

Pu is shrewd. For legal purposes, he has declared himself a pure Sherpa and has claimed Nepalese citizenship, enabling him to export goods, own land, and travel abroad. To the German carpet importers, he says he is Tibetan because that helps to sell carpets. One Tibetan commented, "Pu Kelsang until very recently was a full Tibetan and now he is a full Sherpa. So that's how it is. People are people."

He has done well, he says, because of his ability to design carpets that appeal to Europeans. "Now carpets have become like a fashion business," he said. "Every three to four months we have to change the design. To tell what is fashionable, you have to be in the market to see what kind of color combination and design they like." He exports few carpets to the United States because Americans prefer busier designs and brighter colors. Elaborate designs are more difficult and costly to weave, and the Swiss dye needed for the colors is so expensive that it is more difficult to make a profit.

*   *   *   *   *

Ugen Tsering, Mr. Thinley, and Pu Kelsang are all quite wealthy; they are typical of the growing number of Tibetan entrepreneurs in the Kathmandu valley. In the winter in India, many Tibetans travel to the northern towns to sell sweaters. They sit by the side of the road and display their goods on the ground. In Kathmandu, however, one rarely finds a Tibetan selling merchandise from the roadside; most refugees who are not involved with the government-in-exile factories either rent their own shops or have their own factories. Many of the weavers trained in the CTC-HCE group left the centers in the late 1970s after they had adjusted to life in Nepal. At that time it was still fairly easy to open private carpet shops, restaurants, and weaving factories. Unlike the situation in India, Tibetans in Nepal did not need any legal document or down payment to open their stores. As Tibetans working in the center factories see the success of those entering private business, they follow their path. These entrepreneurs gather regularly with the entire Tibetan community for the various Tibetan holidays, and they look upon the Tibetan government-in-exile as their government. They are loosely organized, with appointed group leaders who serve as channels though which the office of home affairs in Dharmsala can maintain contact.

The carpet trade has provided the Tibetans in Nepal with the unique opportunity to specialize in an economic activity that was not found in Nepal; they have created a new industry that is "distinctly Tibetan" (Gombo 1975:319). Because all members of the community can be involved in carpet weaving, the business has made remaining in a Tibetan community economically feasible. Tibetans can continue living in homogeneous groups where they can maintain their traditional ways of life and retain their "political ideology and goals" (Gombo 1975:306).

Economically, however, their fate is interwoven with the political and economic fate of Nepal. Tibetans have encountered little business competition in Nepal because the country's greatest natural resource – the Himalaya Mountains – has attracted so many tourists. However, they must deal with the frustrations of doing business under a government in which they have no voice. For legal purposes – to obtain export permits, an international passport and the right to own land – Tibetans must apply for Nepalese citizenship. "I am a Nepalese citizen and everyone in my family is," a young Tibetan girl said. "Of course, for paperwork we've got to be Nepalese to buy land or anything, but of course we're not Nepalese, we're Tibetan." In 1985 the Nepalese government enacted a law allowing foreigners to take only one carpet per person through customs. This limitation dealt a serious blow to small-scale shop owners who depend on tourist sales for their survival. When the Nepalese government imposes restrictions on the import of wool, the Tibetans suffer; if it raises taxes, even though Tibetans will not reap the benefits, they must pay them. If anything destabilizes the Nepalese government, the future of these Tibetans, regardless of their loyalty to the Dalai Lama and Tibet, will follow that of Nepal. A dispute between India and Nepal in April 1989 led to an embargo on all but essential trade from India to Nepal. Due to the lack of kerosene, few tourists are traveling to Nepal, transportation is increasingly difficult, and basic necessities, such as flour and sugar, are becoming more and more scarce. What has for the Nepalese become a statement of their independence from India is for the Tibetans simply an economic, and potentially a political, nightmare.

To better represent their interests, Tibetan community leaders formed a Carpet Trading Association in 1983. This organization, headed by Wangchuck Tsering, who retired from government-in-exile service in 1982, consists of managers from the government-in-exile factories and from the larger private companies. They meet regularly to discuss the price and supply of wool, import and export regulations, and any other problems the industry faces.

The Tibetans who have enjoyed this rapid economic advancement are the most visible refugees in Nepal. Their shops, guesthouses, and restaurants line the streets of the towns' tourist sections. Some of them are as wealthy as the middle and upper classes in Nepalese society. They do not represent the fate of the majority of Tibetans in Nepal, however. Of the 14,000 refugees who have settled in Nepal, 6,000 are in the Kathmandu valley. The remaining 8,000 have either gathered to live in the Tibetan settlements set up by aid organizations and the Tibetan government-in-exile outside of the Kathmandu valley or are scattered along the northern border of Nepal where they continue to live in much the same way that they did in Tibet.

The Tibetan businesspeople in Kathmandu have stylishly cut short hair and smooth skin and wear leather jackets and blue jeans imported from Hong Kong. Tibetan horse traders living along the border in western Nepal have long hair and rough, gnarled hands and dress in second-hand clothing. As the fate of the refugees in the Kathmandu valley has been influenced by the expanding economy of Nepal, so has the fate of refugees in remote settlements been guided by environmental and social factors unique to their areas. Distinct characteristics which have evolved in each community must be looked at individually to understand the diversity of the refugee experience in Nepal.

*   *   *   *   *

Yeshi, a short, husky, 63-year-old Tibetan with white hair and a small mustache, was dressed in shabby Western clothes when he attended the settlement meeting by the big, stone schoolhouse in Dhorpatan in the summer of 1986. The residents of Dhorpatan had been called on by Tsering

Choedak, the settlement manager, to discuss their complaints and to hear for the first time the speech read by the Dalai Lama during the celebrations on Tibetan Uprising Day several months earlier. They had also come together to share their memories of the early days in Dhorpatan. Yeshi, one of the first settlers and the most talkative in the group, started off.

At the age of 36, he joined 50 others from the village of Garon in Tibet and escaped during the night. Instead of bringing livestock and personal belongings, they rescued statues, thankhas, and prayer books from their village monastery. Their journey was a disaster: only six or seven people eventually made it to the Nepal border, and all of the precious religious items were lost in flight or stolen by the attacking Chinese army. Several months later, the small band of survivors finally struggled across the same snowy pass into Mustang that Tashi Dhundup and his family had crossed earlier that year. By this time hundreds of refugees were camped in Jomson, eking out whatever livings they could; the area couldn't support any more. The fugitives decided to try their luck farther south and headed down to Pokhara. There they were simply told to continue on to Kathmandu, where it was rumored that more aid was being distributed and a settlement had been established. In Kathmandu, however, the Swiss were overwhelmed with refugees trying to enter Jawalakhel, the only camp in the Kathmandu valley, and they asked Yeshi and his friends to join two other groups and head back west to settle in a new site selected in the Dhorpatan valley.

Dhorpatan, believed to have once been a lake, lies in the middle of a broad, flat valley at 10,000 feet above sea level. It is a five- to six-day trek northwest from Pokhara along the low river valley of the Kali Gandaki. Farther north this river cuts the deepest gorge in the world when it passes between the peaks of Annapurna and Dhaulagiri, each hovering just over 26,000 feet. Even this far south where the altitude is only 3,000 feet, the river carves out a wide canyon that drops steeply and abruptly from the flat, fertile plateau above. On the final day of the trek to the Dhorpatan valley, the trail climbs up through a thick forest, where it is said thieves lie in wait for solo travelers, to an 11,000-foot pass, the Jaljala. Every October, on leaving Dhorpatan to winter in Kathmandu, and every May on his return to the camp, Tsering Choedak hangs new green, blue, and red prayer flags from a pine tree by the side of the trail. Beneath the tree lies a pile of rocks blackened by the pine bows he burns as he prays each season. It is a five-hour walk from the pass to Dhorpatan.

This valley was discovered by Toni Hagen and Peter Aufschnaiter on one of their treks searching for refugees in need of help. Its altitude, cold climate, opportunities for grazing horses and sheep, and lack of local inhabitants made it an ideal spot for resettling Tibetans. Most likely the foreigners passed through on a sunny day, for when the clouds roll in the area suddenly becomes hostile and lonely. The two rows of 13,000-foot hills rising sharply from either side of the valley lose their splendor and become menacing barriers reinforcing the sense of isolation and desolation.

A Swiss staff soon joined Yeshi and the 13 others who had arrived in Dhorpatan in early 1961. The small group camped at the far end of the valley and began their first task, clearing a flat area near the tents for an airstrip. The Royal Nepal Airline Company lent the Swiss its planes and pilots until the foreigners acquired their own plane, a Pilatus Porters flown by a retired Swiss air force captain. After the airstrip was completed, the refugees built one-story stone huts on a slight rise above the river, where the pines would offer some protection from the weather.

ICRC staff in Dhorpatan included a project manager who oversaw the relief program, a nurse, an agricultural specialist, a radio operator, a carpenter who ran a saw mill, a Sherpa translator, and a Tibetan health assistant. The Swiss immediately established a clinic, housed in a pungent-smelling, yak skin tent until a small stone building could be built, where 40 to 60 patients were seen each day. Rice, powdered milk, dhal, and other necessities were airlifted four times a day to Dhorpatan.

Accustomed to a nomadic lifestyle, the Tibetans in Dhorpatan showed little interest in the agricultural projects introduced by the Swiss. Since a handicraft center was impractical in such a remote area, the Swiss decided to buy 30 yak and 51 horses from Dolpo to set up a transport business that would enable the refugees to earn their living by trading as they had in Tibet. The Tibetans were also given buffalo, cows, sheep, and goats, and ICRC provided materials for those who wanted to work as blacksmiths, silversmiths, or carpenters. A cheese factory was opened, too. The refugees wore clothing sent by the stray American tourists who passed through the valley.

As word spread that aid was being distributed in Dhorpatan, refugees who were starving and dying in Dolpo and Mustang on the northwest border of Nepal flocked there. The population, grew from a mere 14 in 1961 to 800 by 1963. The tiny plane could not ferry enough food for the increased numbers, yet larger planes were unable to land safely on the airstrip. To ease the problems created by this overpopulation, the Swiss combined the five villages in the camp into two groups, and announced that one group would move to Pokhara where there was an airstrip for larger planes near another settlement established by the Swiss, Tashi Palkhiel.

The Tibetans, however, were all very happy in Dhorpatan. They felt the Swiss were taking good care of them. They liked the climate in the valley because it was similar to that of Tibet (like most Tibetans at that time, they were afraid of the heat in lower valleys). To make matters worse, the Tibetans in Dhorpatan were, and continue to be, notorious among other refugees for their "roughness" and their inability to get along with others. For five or six days, both groups refused to leave. Finally the Swiss had several policeman from Pokhara flown out to the camp. It was decided that the two Tibetan leaders would determine which group would have to move by a throw of dice. Even then, however, the Tibetans refused to leave. Finally, after some force and persuasion by the Nepalese police, approximately 200 people packed their bedrolls and any remaining valuables onto their ponies and set out for the 15-day trek to Pokhara.

Toward the end of 1961, another group in Dhorpatan decided to leave for India. Compared to the extensive resettlement program in India, very little had been done for the refugees in Nepal and, by this time, no long term plans had been made for them. Many Tibetans stopped only briefly in Nepal before continuing on to India. Many young men went to join the then secret-Tibetan division of the Indian army. Others were afraid the Chinese would enter Nepal, and felt they would be safer farther away. The determining factor, however was that the Dalai Lama had settled in India. By 1962 it was estimated that 10,000 refugees — half of those who had entered Nepal — had migrated to India. The Indian government told the Tibetans to stay in Nepal, stressing that it was also an independent country and that they could settle there. Later on, in 1962, as a result of the Sino-Indian conflict along the Indian-Tibetan border, the Indian border was completely closed — any Tibetan refugees who tried to enter were detained at the border.

As these groups migrated to India, the settlement at Dhorpatan — only recently overflowing with refugees — was almost completely empty. Not wanting to see all their efforts go to waste, the Swiss welcomed back the group sent to Pokhara the previous year. With the population problem finally settled, the Swiss could begin concentrating on helping this group of refugees become self-sufficient.

The next problem the Swiss encountered, which was common in all of the remote settlements, was the question of land ownership. When Hagen and Aufschnaiter had scouted out the Dhorpatan area, the valley was deserted. As soon as the Tibetans began clearing the trees and building houses, however, Nepalese began showing up out of nowhere to claim it as their own property. To help clarify the situation, His Majesty's Government of Nepal and ICRC came to an agreement with the supposed local landowners over land use in the valley. Because the land tenure was not legally documented, the arrangement simply created misunderstandings with the local inhabitants and a sense of insecurity among the refugees. An agreement signed on 24 November 1964 by the Nepalese and Swiss governments called for the Nepalese government to purchase this land.

Land disputes over grazing in the high pastures above the valley, however, still continue to crop up due to the increasing number of people and animals vying for a limited amount of pasture land. Although at one time pasture lands were nationalized by the Nepal government, the local people immediately complained that they were still paying property taxes. The Swiss then arranged for a seven-year lease on a piece of grazing land for the Tibetans, which worked until the lease expired and the problem simply resurfaced. In 1986, Tsering Choedak, the manager of Dhorpatan, was hopeful that an agreement he had reached with the local district officials the previous year would still be upheld.

The Swiss continued to pour money into Dhorpatan; according to one Tibetan, they contributed more to this camp than any other. Things never worked out as the foreigners hoped, however. After three or four years the yak bought to use in the trading business died of liver flukes. The refugees in this region were given 350 acres of land for 350 people; they wanted to trade, however, not to farm. A cooperative was established with contributions from the employees, but the accounts never balanced correctly. In a letter to the director of UNHCR, the Dalai Lama's representative in Nepal recommended that a hotel be built to attract tourists to the area's natural beauty. Local Tibetans suggested that the hotel be a long, one-story stone building similar to those scattered throughout the valley. Instead, at the foreigners' insistence, a modern, two-story hotel with large glass windows overlooking the valley and a fireplace in every room was designed by a German architect; it was built to appeal to those tourists who may have hoped to find the Alps hidden in the Himalayas.

Few tourists visit Dhorpatan, however. Dolpo, the main potential trekking attraction in this region, is a restricted area into which only a handful of applicants get permission to travel—most trekkers choose to go elsewhere. The manager of the cooperative hotel and shop apparently was also interested in going elsewhere: he soon left for India with a 10,000-rupee profit. The hotel now stands empty, broken windows flapping in the wind, an embarrassment to Tibetans and Swiss alike.

The Swiss, who come from a small country where survival depends on one's ability to work with others, thought cooperative stores would work wonderfully in Tibetan settlements. Tibetans, on the other hand, coming from the harsh climate and sparsely populated Tibetan plateau, had learned that to survive, they had to look out for themselves. They neither liked nor understood the idea of paying money to buy stock in a store jointly owned by the community. The co-op has ceased to operate in Dhorpatan; while these stores are permanent fixtures in many of the other settlements, they generate little profit.

The smuggling of religious icons from Tibet still divides the settlement. Two groups evolved in the camp: the insiders, who used force to ensure they were the first to receive aid, and the outsiders, who got the leftovers. The insiders, who are generally involved in the smuggling, continue to dominate; they build new houses and purchase hand-woven, wool saddle blankets for their large herds of ponies; their wives flaunt silver necklaces, belts, and headpieces studded with turquoise, coral, and *tzi.* The outsiders, by contrast, survive on potatoes and struggle to afford butter for their tea.

Despite the difficulties, most Tibetans in Dhorpatan have been able to earn a living by transporting goods on horses. In April and May, the refugees plant their fields with seed potatoes left over from the previous year. Teenagers head to the high pastures to spend the summer grazing their families' herds. Toward the end of the summer, when the potatoes are being harvested, the shepherds come down from the pasture land and begin preparations for their journey to the Terai. Except for those too old or sick to travel, the entire population in the Dhorpatan valley, both Tibetan and Nepalese, leaves during the bitter winter months and travels to the Terai. The traders will make as many trips as possible while the trail is still passable so that they can earn enough to support their family during the winter. They sleep in rented rooms and spin wool, and graze their herds of ponies on land rented from local residents. As spring approaches, the traders arrange jobs transporting rice and other grains north into the mountains, and the cycle begins anew.

*   *   *   *   *

Although the worlds of the entrepreneur and the horse trader seem far apart, the news of financial success in the increasingly Westernized Kathmandu valley slowly makes its way to even the most remote village. Carried by porters and discussed quietly over smoky fires, the allure of the material West tugs at almost each and every Tibetan, especially the young. And so the success, or lack thereof, in the businessperson's ability to maintain his or her Tibetan culture is a vision for the future cultural identity of all Tibetans. It is a future that is rapidly becoming the present.

Part Three

Preserving the Ideal

> By preserving our traditions and history and having a separate language and culture we can prove to the world that Tibet is free.
> —*Wangdu Chodak, teacher, the Atisha School*

> Say Tibet doesn't get its independence and we will still be living outside Tibet, then my children will be the third generation. They may not be working for the Tibetan government, they may be working for the government of Nepal, an international organization, or a private factory. Whatever they are doing, they should still be keeping their traditions, they should still consider themselves Tibetans. This is, I think, very important for them—to think of themselves as Tibetans. They must know that they do not belong to the place where they are living now, they belong somewhere else and that place is called Tibet.
> —*Karma, secretary, Snow Lion Foundation*

Chapter 7

Prayer Wheels and Stupas

> Tibetans cherish their culture because in Buddhism they have the knowledge of how to seek and obtain a permanent happiness, a happiness that is more encompassing than that which concerns this life. We cherish Tibetan Buddhism and Tibetan Buddhism means His Holiness the Dalai Lama.
>
> — *Gelek Rinpoche*

The Buddha's birthday, 1986: Laughter floats up through the gray, early-morning light; downstairs, a kerosene stove begins to hum. The metal door to the outhouse scrapes against the rocky ground. Somewhere a Hindu begins to pray to his gods, pounding drums and ringing bells as he chants from the depths of his soul. Tsering, a slight, 35-year-old Tibetan woman, has been awake for more than an hour making potato curry and chapatis for our outing.

Lobsang Nyima, her husband, shuffles through the house murmuring prayers while he fills the seven silver bowls on the altar with water, as he does every morning as an offering to the gods. No matter how poor a family nor how run-down the home, every Tibetan household has an area set aside as an altar. A photograph of the Dalai Lama with a respectful white *khatag* (scarf) draped over the frame is the focal point of each shrine. Drawings or small statues of the Buddha, occasional offerings of food, and butter lamps (which are slowly being replaced by less expensive electric bulbs where there is electricity) fill the remaining space.

By 7:30, prayers and preparation are complete, and we set out for Bodnath to celebrate the Buddha's birthday. The golden spire of the Bodnath stupa dominates the horizon on the northeastern edge of Kathmandu. The penetrating eyes of the stupa, representating *yeshe*, the ability to discern the ultimate nature of reality, gaze out across the green rice fields of the valley.

On the Buddha's birthday, a day set aside for personal worship and for improving one's own store of karma, the base of the stupa is crowded with pilgrims circling the dome, fingering wooden prayer beads, chanting "Om Mani Padme Hum," and hanging brilliant blue, white, red, green, and yellow prayer flags to represent sky, clouds, fire, water, and earth. Prayer flags are called *lung tda* in Tibetan, which literally translates as "wind horse": they symbolize "the swiftness and deliberateness with which the wind carries the prayers to the Buddha's realm" (Gold 1984:26). Scores of these flags now hang in clusters, flapping gently in the occasional breeze.

On the ground level, beneath the dome of the stupa, more worshipers circle around and around, giving alms to the poor, gossiping with their neighbors, and spinning ancient prayer wheels of silver and copper, inside of which are attached printed mantra sheets. Spinning prayer wheels invoke the mantras within and multiply the number of prayers sent to the gods. Larger, more elaborate wheels are found in monasteries or in streams where they will constantly revolve and thus bring a steady flow of good merit to the builders.

"Are such prayers and recitations due merely to custom, are they mere rituals to embellish daily life?" the Dalai Lama asks. "The answer is definitely negative, because controlling and disciplining the mind is or should be the primary purpose of all prayers and religious recitations" (Dalai Lama 1980:37). The act is important only insofar as it serves as a manifestation of that internal motivation to increase one's mindfulness. A Buddhist thinker says,

> The Tibetans are not out to "cheat the gods" by placating them with sham prayers, or to escape the trouble of exerting himself and escaping the responsibility for his own deeds and conduct (karma). Prayers in the Buddhist sense are the calling up of the forces that dwell within ourselves and that can only be effective if we are free from selfish desires. . . . Buddhists do not put their faith in the power of gods, residing in some heavens beyond, but they believe in the power of motive and the purity of faith, the purity of intention. (Govinda 1970:22)

After circling the stupa three times, Nyima donates half of a month's salary to provide a kilo of gold dye for decorating the dome, and we enter the small, brick monastery of the Tibetan government-in-exile.

Inside the monastery it is dark and smoky. Thousands of candles flicker on the altar and the air is thick with the heavy smell of butter rising from the butter lamps lit by each visitor. A huge statue of Padma Sambhava, the legendary Indian saint who overcame the spirits of the Bon religion and introduced Buddhism into Tibet in the eighth century, towers over the room from his seat at the center of the altar. Faded, century-old thankhas hang from the ceiling, and prayer books carried down from Tibet lie in alcoves built on either side of the center statues. Near the altar are two raised chairs draped with maroon cloths, where the Rinpoche and the abbot of the monastery sit. They lead the monks in prayer, stopping intermittently to give blessings to the steady stream of worshipers.

The chants and prayers of 30 or so maroon-and-saffron-clad monks rise up from two low, cushioned benches. Five- and six-year-old boys scratch, wiggle, and stare at the Buddhist pilgrims, but shaven-headed teenage students and older, gray-haired monks pray with concentration and emotion. As one section of the liturgy draws to a close, the chanting intensifies and the pace quickens; suddenly the deep, eerie call of the long horns resounds through the *gonpa* (monastery). The horns are joined by the muffled bass notes of the drums and the high-pitched rattle of small, one-handled wooden drums, Finally, cymbals crash, conch shells are blown, and the entire gonpa vibrates with the soul-stirring music.

> Tibetan ritual music is built upon the deepest vibrations that an instrument or a human voice can produce: sounds that seem to come from the womb of the earth or from the depth of space like rolling thunder . . . and which symbolize the creative vibrations of the universe, the origin of all things. (Govinda 1970:60)

Then, as abruptly as it had begun, the music stops. The monks readjust their robes, turn the pages of their long, rectangular prayer books, and take a sip of cooled-off tea, thick with butter, from the wooden cups at their knees.

As the monks pray, Lobsang pours melted butter from a blue, metal pitcher carried from home into several large butter lamps, and we each light smaller lamps on the altar for our continued well-being.

Outside in the bright sun and heat we head toward the next gonpa. The Tibetans chat with acquaintances as we pay our respects to the different monasteries, receive the blessings of the various Rinpoches, and spin the prayer wheels set in the stone walls along the connecting paths. Later that afternoon we head across town to the stupa at Swayambhunath. After visiting the stupa, Tenzin — Lobsang and Tsering's four-year-old son — and I climb the steps to a smaller gonpa set up on a knoll. We peer through the window into a dark room crowded with older men and women dressed in heavy wool chubbas, chanting "Om Mani Padme Hum" and prostrating again and again. They kneel down, stretch out full-length on the floor with their hands in a praying motion above their head and then pull themselves

One hundred and forty-six monasteries have been built in India and Nepal as the refugees struggle to keep Tibetan Buddhism alive in exile. This monk entered the Khumbu Valley in 1960 and is now the oldest monk in the monastery at Chialsa. ©Ann Forbes

back to an upright position. "Prostration," writes Geshe Dhargyey, "is one of the strongest opponent forces of pride since it is a form of surrendering" (Dhargyey and Rapten 1977:83). We later pass worshipers, hands and knees padded, who had spent the entire day prostrating themselves around and around the three-kilometer road ringing the base of the stupa as they work to increase their store of good merit and improve their chances in the next incarnation.

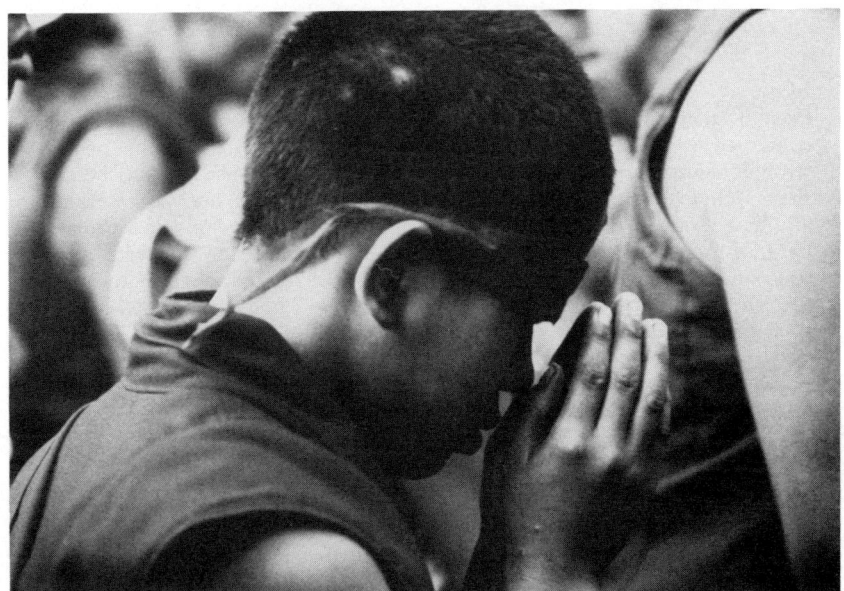

In Tibet every family sends at least one son to join a monastery. Although this practice is less rigid in exile, children often enter the monastery when they are very young and are expected to continue as monks for the remainder of their lives.
©Peter Forbes

Tenzin and I rejoin the family and walk down a cool, shady path to a smaller stone stupa where a large crowd has gathered on a cement platform built against the hill. Because Lobsang Nyima works for the government-in-exile, we are shown to the front, where we sit on cushions on the ground and are served a lukewarm cup of butter tea. Shortly thereafter the crowd silences itself with loud whispers and everyone stands up. A revered lama walks down the hill and takes his place on the slightly raised cushion at the front of the crowd. Everyone bows silently and we sit back down. The praying now commences in full force. On my right sits Tsering, the mother, who concentrates on preventing her children from spilling tea, talking, or fighting. On my left sits a 28-year-old schoolteacher in tinted sunglasses, his eyes shut in concentration as he chants the prayers led by the lama.

Forty-five minutes later, as the sun begins to slip behind the hills, the prayers come to a close and the worshipers prepare to leave. We walk back by the prostrating pilgrims and wait in a long line for a cab back to Jawalakhel.

* * * * *

Even if such important factors as culture and heritage are excluded, the continued well-being of the monasteries is a necessity. Tibetan people strongly depend on religion as a source of comfort and consolation. Tibetans are psychologically sound and practical people. They are hard-working and have come through countless hardships with little psychological damage because they feel they are backed by people who they know have a more profound understanding of the world than themselves and to whom they can turn in time, who lead a life which they too may choose and which brings strong inner peace — once worldly life is seen as senseless. Thus, although many people remain mainly concerned with their worldly obligations and interests, psychologically they need to feel that religious institutions are strong. (Tibet Society and Relief Fund 1985)

Tibetan Buddhism was the foundation of Tibetan culture as it existed on the Tibetan plateau before the Chinese invasion. By the time of the invasion, monasteries had become the country's greatest social and economic force; every secular official was mirrored by a monk, and the country was ruled by the reincarnation of a god. The Tibetan national flag, introduced by the 13th Dalai Lama in 1912, shows two snow lions holding the three jewels of Buddhism — the Buddha, the Dharma (the law), and the Sangha (the monastic community) — before a 12-rayed sun rising up over a snow-capped peak.

Spiritually as well as physically, the monasteries housed the Buddhist doctrine for Tibet. Individuals struggling on their own to live within the laws of Buddhism depended on the support and guidance of these institutions. "Monasteries," the Dalai Lama's sister explains, "were places where anyone could come anytime to pray and seek spiritual guidance. They were also places of learning and religious practices — where prayer, meditation, and the practice of good and the avoidance of evil had become a way of life." They provided the foundation for the security of individual Tibetans as well as for the stability of the community, and they offered almost the only organized education in the country.

All of the physical manifestations — the icons, monasteries, and stupas — of Tibetan Buddhism were almost completely obliterated during the Chinese invasion and the subsequent Cultural Revolution. Had it not been for the Dalai Lama and the 100,000 Tibetans who followed him across the high peaks into exile, the Chinese would also have come close to wiping out the spiritual heart of Buddhism in Tibet.

Recognizing that the future of Vajrayana Buddhism, the branch of Buddhism practiced in its pure form only in Tibet, was endangered, the Dalai Lama immediately set out to lay a foundation for its survival in exile. As soon as arrangements could be made, monks in India were sent to a camp in Buxa Duar, where rations of rice and powdered milk were distributed. Those who were well enough began rewriting the scriptures before they were forgotten or before those who knew them died of the tuberculosis that threatened the entire monastic community. Monks arriving in the Kathmandu valley initially gathered at the stupas in Boudha and Swayambhu with other members of their monastery and begged for food. Some monks were able to earn a few rupees by performing the only skill they had—reading scriptures in the rooms of Tibetans and local Sherpas or Tamangs. Father Moran's committee distributed rice, dhal, flour, and powdered milk among the monks and nuns for one year, but the organization already had its hands full assisting refugees in other parts of Nepal. Father Moran contacted the Nepalese Buddhist Society, which eventually agreed to assume the responsibility for administering assistance to the monastic community.

As the refugees began to earn money, the lay population was able to support the monastic communities in India and Nepal by calling upon monks to read prayers or perform other ceremonies in their homes. Although Tibetans are reluctant to donate money to a school or a hospital, they usually give enthusiastically to monasteries, and in the late 1960s and early 1970s they began contributing funds for the reconstruction of the Tibetan monasteries in exile. By 1986 there were 146 new monasteries, 35 of which are in Nepal, and there are now approximately 6,500 monks and 350 nuns living in exile. The large monasteries of Tibet—Drepung, Sera and Ganden—were rebuilt in southern India, where they continue to maintain their historically high standard of philosophical schooling. In addition to the monasteries, the Institute of Higher Tibetan Studies was founded in 1968 in Benares as a special wing of the Varanasi Sanskrit University, and the Buddhist School of Dialectics was opened in 1973 in Dharmsala.

*   *   *   *   *

Monasteries in exile continue to serve as the spiritual backbone of the Tibetan community; they have provided the Tibetans with a continuity and stability vital to their successful adjustment as refugees. The monastic life, although not for everyone, is still looked upon as the most honorable path in life. The religious leaders of Tibetan Buddhism—the Dalai Lama, the heads of the four religious sects, and certain reincarnate lamas—serve as the spiritual guides for both the lay and the religious populations. Lay Buddhists recognize the superior wisdom of these leaders and look to them for guidance in interpreting the tenets of Buddhist philosophy and applying them to everyday life. They seek out monks to read scriptures, provide advice, and perform elaborate ceremonies to ward off potential evil spirits. These functions in turn range from those involving the strictest application of Buddhist philosophy to decisions and actions which are a combination of Bon magic, Buddhist practices, and superstition.

Tsering Dolkar, the woman in whose home I lived for a year, once had a bad dream about having her teeth pulled out. She consulted a lama, who interpreted the dream as a sign that her husband's elderly aunt in Tibet was sick and recommended that certain prayers be read to help cure her. Although Tsering was unable to verify this information, the family immediately called several lamas to her home to read the prescribed scriptures. When stricken with a boil above my eye, the schoolchildren told me to go to a lama so he could blow on it and say a mantra because, they explained, "lamas understand everything." Another time, the family with whom I was living was worried when I was late returning from a field trip; they consulted a monk who assured them that I would return on the fourth day, which, in fact, was correct.

It is difficult to generalize regarding who seeks the advice of lamas for such decisions and who prefers to reach their own conclusions. "Oh, yeah, we have a Rinpoche in Swayambhu," said a young, very Westernized Tibetan girl who manages her family's trekking shop in Thamel.

> He's a real nice Rinpoche and any problems we have we go to him. My mother is *very* into that, any problem, anything she finds superstitious, dreams, anything, she'll go to him. I don't go all that much because I tell my mom, "Geez, that's a dream; it won't happen," but she doesn't listen. She tells me I must go talk to him. Sometimes I just go and I'll sit for a half hour, an hour, and talk to him and he'll tell you things and it makes you feel better, so I'm glad I go. I go sometimes, but I don't go that often.

A young Tibetan carpet exporter, who was educated in a missionary school in India, offered a different perspective when describing *mo*:

> Mo is an old custom, still we do it. If I was going to travel to India or to Europe, I would go to a lama to see if it is good or bad for me to travel. If it's okay than maybe I will go. He might also say okay, but you should do such-and-such prayers in a monastery. If you want to go, it is better for you to have these prayers done.

Karma, a Tibetan in Kathmandu, has worked for the Tibetan government since he was 15 years old. His job satisfies his social conscience, yet it does not provide him with economic security. He is now married and has two young daughters. Because he realizes how valuable an education is, he sent his oldest, Chokyi, to an English medium nursery school rather than to the school in the nearby refugee settlement, and he opened a carpet shop in hope of raising enough money to send his daughters to a private school in India. A foreign friend offered to assist him in paying the school fees, which were far beyond what Karma could ever hope to earn even from his government job and carpet shop combined. Karma gratefully accepted and made plans to go to India to seek admission for his child. Two days later, he informed the foreigner that he no longer needed his assistance, that his daughter would remain in Nepal and attend a Tibetan settlement school. Looking back on his decision, he said:

> I think it is very difficult for Westerners to understand. I want Chokyi to become somebody — a doctor or a lawyer or a writer, something that she can do by herself. I thought if I sent her to a high-standard English school rather than a settlement school, there would be a better chance of accomplishing this. If she could go to an English school, she would not study Tibetan language and history; but if she could become something, then that would be okay, I would be happy. On the other hand, if she was not a good student, if she couldn't become a doctor or a lawyer and she also lost her Tibetanness, she would have nothing. That would be very bad, it would all have been a waste.
>
> The expense for such a school is beyond my capacity so when I heard of my friend's willingness to sponsor her, I felt very happy and I thought I should find a school right away. Before I left I consulted two lamas to have them read mo. Both times the mo said it was better for Tsering Chokyi to stay in Nepal, so I dropped the whole idea and planned to send her to the Tibetan school in Tashi Palkhiel.

*   *   *   *   *

In exile, the monastic community provides an essential link with the past. More important, it serves as a link with the spiritual world: through their daily practices religious leaders act as vehicles through which the wisdom of enlightenment can enter the lives of laypeople. Their advice does not simply assist a refugee in making a particular decision; it assures Tibetans that they are not alone, that there is something more powerful, more profound than individual actions and solitary people. Through their understanding of and connection with the spiritual world, religious leaders are thus able to offer guidance that is seen as deeper and more enduring than anything that outsiders or secular leaders could ever provide.

And yet Tibetan Buddhism provides more than solace and direction. Tibetan Buddhism is a way of life; its values constitute the framework through which Tibetans make sense of, find meaning in, and act in the world. The fusion of the secular and spiritual worlds is personified in the structure of the Tibetan government-in-exile, which has placed one of the highest religious leaders of Tibetan Buddhism as the head of the state.

More than 300,000 Buddhists journeyed to Bodh Gaya in December 1985 to attend the Kalachakra Initiation and to receive the blessing of the 14th Dalai Lama of Tibet. Here the Dalai Lama is receiving a kha tag during the ceremony.
©Ann Forbes

Tenzin Gyatso, the 14th Dalai Lama and thus the ruler of Tibet, is first and foremost a monk; his political decisions arise from a profound understanding of the world that has been gleaned from years of religious study. His actions are based neither on spiritual rhetoric nor on his spontaneous reaction to the briefings of advisors. Rather, his statements and policies are derived from his own careful exploration of the particular issue from within the framework of Tibetan Buddhism.

Although not all Tibetans adhere strictly to the Buddhist path, all support the Dalai Lama. They listen attentively to his words and they follow his advice as best they can. In this way, through the Dalai Lama, the values of Buddhism are reflected in the social and political actions of the entire community; the Buddhist ideals espoused by and embodied in their leader set the ethical code for the lay population.

Unlike Western political thought, which typically centers on resolving the differences between humans and groups of humans, between majorities and minorities, the Dalai Lama emphasizes the basic equality and unity of all sentient beings. Everyone wants to be at peace and to obtain happiness;

no one wants to suffer. The Dalai Lama calls on his followers to look first for this underlying unity in understanding the actions of others, and in working to resolve conflict. To this end, in both his religious teachings and his political actions he reiterates the importance of developing compassion for others — even for one's greatest enemies — and of assuming a sense of responsibility for the outcomes of our actions. He explains:

> Today the world is smaller and smaller and more interdependent. One nation's problems can no longer be solved by itself completely. Thus without a sense of universal responsibility, our very survival is threatened. Basically, universal responsibility is feeling for other people's suffering just as we feel for our own. It is the realization that even our enemy is entirely motivated by the quest for happiness. We must recognize that all human beings want the same things we want. (Dalai Lama 1980:19)

Though his role as a world leader is derived solely from his position as a Buddhist leader, the Dalai Lama is realistic about this source of power and about the role that Buddhism can play in others' lives. He lives by the example that religion — any religion — is only as powerful as the heart of the person who believes in it. Without honesty and sincerity, without compassion, all things — knowledge, technology, and even religion — simply become useless and destructive.

> A religious person may be a very good scholar, but if the motivation is negative, is improper, then religion itself becomes destructive. Then religion, one means of eliminating human suffering, becomes another instrument to bring more suffering and division among human beings. (Dalai Lama, personal communication, 1986)

Any effort to ease the plight of the world must thus start with the individual, with each human working to become more honest, more sincere, and more compassionate.

Most remarkable, perhaps, the Dalai Lama refuses to express hostility toward the Chinese, even in light of the recent brutal repression in Tibet, and he finds positive ramifications in his predicament as an exiled leader with no real land and no real power. The Chinese invaded his homeland, destroying his country and much of its heritage. In their actions, he says, they forced him actually to carry out and live by the Buddhist philosophy of compassion to one's enemies. This experience in turn has enhanced his own spiritual understanding and has helped him to be a better guide for other Tibetans and for other human beings.

> In the past there was too much formality. You couldn't talk, you couldn't even breathe freely. . . . I hate being formal. In this way, you see, becoming a refugee was actually useful. It brought me much closer to reality. And also it deepened my understanding of religion, particularly impermanence. Although the world is always changing one never notices it. Then suddenly

your home, your friends and country all are gone. It showed how futile it is to hold on to such things. (Dalai Lama, quoted in Avedon 1984:71)

Few lay practitioners live up to the standard set by their leader; few expect to. Almost all Tibetans, however, do try to understand the advice of the Dalai Lama and to apply it to their daily lives as best as they can. His example serves as the ideal against which they measure their own actions.

Sonam Tsering, principal of the refugee school in the mountainous Solu Khumbu region, lost both his father and mother to the Chinese; he was forced to flee his home and enter Nepal as a beggar. Since then, the Chinese have systematically worked to obliterate his culture and his religion; they have murdered his compatriots and stripped away the rights of his leader. Yet, he says, the Chinese are not his enemies. "External enemies are not permanent," Sonam quotes the Dalai Lama. "If you respect him, your enemy will become your friend." "We are our own enemies," Sonam explained.

> We must learn to control the three passions: *timug* (blind passion), *shedang* (anger), and *do chag* (carnal desire), and cut through the clutter of the ego so that the awakening mind, the Buddha mind, can unfold naturally without inhibitions. If we fail to do this, we will bring about a destruction far more permanent than the Chinese can ever inflict. The Chinese can destroy this life; yet only we can ruin our chance for rebirth as a human, and only as humans do we have the opportunity to control our future lives.

One sunny, hot afternoon before distributing report cards and awards at the Atisha Primary School prize day ceremonies, Lobsang Nyima gave a speech on the importance of education in which he offered a more tangible example of the integral role that karma plays in Tibetans' actions in the world. In Tibet, Nyima had been a monk; he had learned to read and write Tibetan and had memorized scores of Tibetan scriptures. After fleeing his country, he studied Buddhist philosophy at the Varanasi Sanskrit University. Subsequently he gave up his monastic vows, married, and began working for the Tibetan government-in-exile.* Nyima has no modern education and he cannot read or write English. As manager of a carpet factory that exports to Europe, he must suddenly depend on his assistants for translation during meetings with foreign importers, for reading and writing his correspondence, and for any overseas travel.

Addressing the illiterate parents and the 135 four-to- fifteen-year-old students, Lobsang Nyima explained that with an education one can stand

---

* Upon entering exile, many Tibetans chose to give up their monastic vows despite the dishonor and negative karma that this action is believed to bring. As refugees and as monks, they felt they were unable to work directly toward regaining independence and helping the Tibetan community. Other monks who had been sent to the monasteries unwillingly also had the opportunity to leave if they wished.

on one's own feet. It is important to study hard even if you are to die the very next day, he said, because an education is the one thing that nothing, not even death, can take away. Those subjects learned in previous incarnations will come more easily in this lifetime because they do not have to be learned all over again—you must simply refresh your memory. Students who are smart are not necessarily more intelligent or better people than others who appear to be more stupid and who must struggle even to pass; the slower students are simply seeing the material for the first time, he explained. To offset any lack of learning in past lives and to ensure success in future lives, he emphasized, it is critical that you work diligently and relentlessly now, every day; you must not waste a minute.

* * * * *

Among so many other peoples without countries, Tibetans are perhaps better equipped to accept their current suffering because of their profound faith in Buddhism. The belief that each individual is responsible for his own soul, that Tibetans are collectively responsible for the future of their country, frees the refugees to concentrate on creating the forces that will bring about eventual liberation—of their spirit and of their country. They focus on what they can do now to work toward their salvation; they do not wait for some god or some nation to release them from this bondage. Just as they will not lose faith if they do not attain enlightenment in this lifetime, the refugees will not give up hope if those now in exile do not live to see a free Tibet. The process to freedom, they know, is long; it takes not one generation or one lifetime, but a thousand generations, a thousand lifetimes.

Chapter 8

Conflicts

> You Americans are looking for Shambhala but nowadays Tibetans want to go to New York City.
> —*Sakya Rinpoche to Edmund Berbaum*, The Way to Shambhala

> The Tibetan lives in a permanent state of anxious uneasiness; every physical or spiritual disturbance, each illness, every uncertain or threatening situation causes him to embark on a feverish search for the cause of the event and the appropriate means to ward it off.
> —*Giuseppe Tucci*, The Religions of Tibet

The *ngag pa* arrived at Tashi's house early in the morning. He was an older man with a head of long, streaked straw matted from years of random neglect. He was dressed in a worn, brown chubba tied over layers and layers of clothing, each layer dirtier than the first. He took off his red and black Tibetan boots, sat cross-legged on the bed, and pulled a tattered prayer book and a wooden tea bowl out from under one of the layers. Wangmo, Tashi's wife, greeted the ngag pa respectfully and poured tea and tsampa into the bowl, which he had placed on the low table set on the bed at his knees. He unwrapped the long, narrow Tibetan prayer book and immediately began chanting from its faded, hand-written pages. This book, he later explained, had been written many, many years ago by his ancestors. He had carried it down from Tibet. Now it was very old, its edges torn and some of the letters defaced. The book should be copied before the prayers were completely lost, he said, but these days people were not interested, and his own eyes were no longer good enough.

When I returned later that day for lunch, the ngag pa was still on the bed praying. While chanting, he made *namkhas*, which were similar to what I made as a child to ward off the "evil eye," by wrapping strands of brightly colored green, blue, and red yarn around two crossed sticks. Outside on the stone wall, Tashi was kneading together a pile of gray mud and water which the ngag pa would need later in the evening. Wangmo was inside heating up dhal over the small mud stove. The ngag pa told them what he would need for that evening's ceremony: chang, tsampa, butter, and pieces of corn.

In Chialsa four children had died of measles in a two week period. Tashi and Wangmo's 10-month-old daughter, Chimney, had had the measles, had recovered, and then suddenly, soon after the fourth death, in their neighbor's home, began having coughing fits that shook her entire body and forced her to spit out globs of thick, yellow mucus. The Tibetan doctor in the settlement prescribed a certain medicine; unlike most Tibetan doctors, however, this doctor was not highly respected and the refugees no longer fully trusted his advice. So Tashi also carried Chimney an hour to the nearest Western hospital, where they prescribed penicillin to treat what was diagnosed as pneumonia.

Many of the Tibetans in the village had what Tashi translated as a doubt, or a suspicion. They feared that something else was involved in the deaths of their children, something that could not be cured by Tibetan or Western medicines alone. They thought that one of the children had not yet given up this world. They whispered that the child's spirit had not entered the *bardo* (world between two existences) in preparation for eventual rebirth, but had instead come under the control of the Lord of Death. In such instances, the spirit becomes what is translated as a "life-cutter"; it wanders the countryside, enters a home, and refuses to leave until it has stolen the soul of one of the occupants to bring to its master. When Tibetans suspect such occurrences, they call upon a monk who is a specialist in astrology to calculate where the spirit has wandered. The monk examines the time of the person's birth and death; if he determines that the spirit has gone to another house, he will specify the number of family members, animals, and rooms in that house. He then tells the family what they must do to satisfy the life-cutter so that the wandering spirit will not take the lives of any members of the house. Actions of appeasement may include reading certain prayers, freeing a chicken or other animal from captivity and thus saving a life, repainting a temple, or, in more serious cases, calling a ngag pa.

After the fourth death in Chialsa, a monk had made calculations to determine where the spirit had gone. Tashi and Wangmo's house fit the description, and, penicillin or no, they called on the ngag pa.

* * * * *

According to Tucci, a renowned Tibetan Buddhist scholar, a ngag pa is an exorcist who engages in a "wide range of activities for the furtherance of good and the defense against evil" (Tucci 1980:172). Another Buddhist monk described a ngag pa as a man who has a certain power that enables him to perform magic. Milarepa, a famous Tibetan poet saint said to have lived in southern Tibet during the eleventh century, had been a ngag pa who used his powers to create hailstorms and fires to destroy his enemies; he later renounced these practices, became a saint, and achieved enlightenment in a single lifetime. With his powers as a ngag pa, Padma Sambhava, the mythological carrier of Buddhism to Tibet, conquered the good and bad deities and protectors that ran freely in Tibet under the Bon religion, establishing a foundation for Buddhism. "While keeping their fear-inspiring character, the deities gave their 'heart' to Padma Sambhava, and promised to be defenders of the Buddhist law" (Tucci 1980:167).

By reciting mantras the ngag pa can call these deities to help him fight the servants of the Lord of Death and thus prevent the occurrence of evil. The ceremony the ngag pa performs is called *Si Lang*. "Si" is translated by Chandra Das (1985) as "a species of devil or demon devouring especially children; a devil bringing misfortune"; "Si Lang" means to press down this devil or this evil spirit.

The actual ability of the ngag pa to exorcise this evil depends both on the "power" that he receives from a lama in an intitiation ceremony and on his later instruction. Following his initiation, the ngag pa spends many years studying the secret practices of tantric Buddhism until his tutor is certain that he is ready to study on his own. After practicing and meditating for several years in solitude, the ngag pa returns to the community and, among other things, begins to perform rituals.

The ngag pa's success or failure at exorcising evil spirits is "like throwing arrows in the dark. Maybe you will hit the target, maybe you won't; it's not quite sure." Tucci (1980:183) said, "the evil powers to be warded off either accept the offering and allow themselves to be appeased, in which case they tacitly reaffirm their promise of obedience to the law, or else they disdain the gifts and prefer to persevere in evil."

Because the training is said to be less rigorous than it once was in Tibet, many Tibetans discredit the work of those ngag pas who continue to practice in exile. These skeptics claim that few retain the power for which famous ngag pas in Tibet are renowned. This skepticism does not imply that the ceremonies themselves can be dismissed as mere superstition, however. In Tucci's opinion, these rituals are to be seen as one of the countless modes of experience of the cosmic illusion; the powers [gods, etc.] addressed in them represent only deceptive products of our own ignorance. At the same time this does not detract from their practical usefulness in a world where the existence of a thing is the same as its imagined existence. (Tucci 1980:177)

Understanding of the tenets of Buddhism can be at various levels, depending on individual capacities. This capacity and thus one's level of understanding, is based on an individual's actions in previous lives. Because no two people's lives, or karmas, are identical, practitioners will necessarily be at different points in their level of comprehension. Although the ceremony of a ngag pa is unnecessary for an advanced yogi who is well on his way to perceiving that all phenomenon in this world are an illusion, it may serve a valuable role for "lay Buddhists . . . whose grade of intellectual faculties does not permit them to escape 'conventional truth' " (Corlin 1975:33).

*   *   *   *   *

When I returned at six o'clock that evening, the lama was back on the bed. Now, instead of reading, he was making the *torma*. The most common tormas are white, conical shapes molded out of rice flour or tsampa and water by monks praying in houses or in monasteries. There are numerous variations, however, and the torma used depends on the prayer being read; some are quite elaborate and take four monks several hours to prepare, and others are quite simple. The monks chant mantras to entice any bad luck or evil spirits residing in the house into the torma. Ceremony complete, the torma is then taken far from the house and destroyed.

The ngag pa now carefully placed the various shapes of the torma in their proper order on a narrow, two-foot-long wooden plank in preparation for the exorcism. At the front end of the plank stood a blue, yellow, and red namkha. Behind this was the figure of an animal sitting back on his haunches with big eyes and a pug nose, molded out of the mud Tashi had prepared earlier in the day. This animal was the leader; its job would be to attract the attention of the spirit struggling to steal the soul of the sick child away to the Lord of Death. A sculpted tiger with the same big, round eyes and flat nose followed the leader, perched upright on top of another four-legged beast. This tiger was the spirit eater; in its paws were the bow and arrows with which to shoot the spirit. An Indian rupee was stuck in its belly for tea money so the spirit would not get thirsty, grains of corn were scattered around to keep it from getting hungry, and a dish of chang was provided to keep it occupied. A third mud creature came at the end to ensure that the spirit did not escape. Lastly, the ngag pa placed a butter lamp at the front edge of the plank to light the path.

The torma complete, the ngag pa took out another, larger prayer book, also yellowed and worn, and began chanting as he unrolled a bell and a *dorje* from a soiled cloth. The dorje, translated as "adamantine diamond" or thunderbolt, symbolizes *shunyata* ("emptiness") and manifests cutting through illusion to the ultimate nature of reality. As the ngag pa worked, he stopped to answer various questions about where the tsampa path should be made on the floor, where the torma should be taken, and who should close the door. He then focused on his chanting.

By this time it was quite dark. The room was lit by only one kerosene lantern held by a wire behind the ngag pa so he could read. Shadows flickered across his lined face as he loudly, then softly, chanted the mantra. The 10-by-15-foot room was barely large enough to hold six people. Chimney lay sleeping peacefully on the bed next to the ngag pa, and Tashi checked her every few minutes to make sure she was all right. Wangmo went back and forth to the kitchen to stir the thukpa; Namgyal, her 23-year-old brother, flipped through the pages of a Hindi magazine; a neighbor who had offered his assistance sat quietly on the edge of the bed.

The ngag pa began chanting more quickly and more vigorously than before. He rang the bell loudly and more frequently, and he rotated the dorje in the air. Suddenly, he stopped. He announced that he was ready and gave final instructions. Again he began loudly reading the mantras, ringing the bell, and moving the dorje continually. The chants abruptly turned into shouts: "Sho! Sho! Sho!" ("Come! Come! Come!"). Shouting, Tashi and Namgyal ran to the door, Namgyal with the board holding the torma and the spirit. A neighbor hacked the bench where the wooden plank had been with a big butcher knife, yelling "Sho! Sho! Sho!" and then ran out the door after the others. Wangmo hastily swept away the trail of tsampa which had led from the spirit catcher to the door, in order to destroy the path back to the room, and then rushed to slam the front door shut. The ngag pa jumped up and threw the bench across the room, yelling loudly for the spirit to leave. The three men could be heard yelling "Sho! Sho! Sho!" as they raced with the torma down the trail. They threw the mud figures into the woods and slashed them, and, symbolically, the spirit, to pieces with the knife.

Inside, all was quiet. The lama pulled on his boots and went outside. Wangmo swept the floor clean, straightened up the room, and wiped out the bowls for the thukpa. Chimney slept peacefully. After a few moments everyone returned. The neighbor assured Tashi and Wangmo that now Chimney would recover quickly. Wangmo served thukpa to everyone, and they discussed why the manager of Chialsa had not yet returned from

Kathmandu.

The next day Chimney seemed much better. She smiled and her cough was less harsh. Tashi and Wangmo said happily that the ngag pa had been successful and we celebrated by eating *mo mo*, a meat dumpling that was an expensive treat in Chialsa. The following day, however, Chimney was much worse; she was up all night coughing; her skin was pale and her eyes dull and lifeless. That afternoon Tashi carried her back to the hospital, where the doctor diagnosed acute pneumonia and, as a last resort, prescribed penicillin injections.

*   *   *   *   *

The following day a 30-year-old Tibetan schoolteacher, raised in Kathmandu and educated in India, rather disdainfully explained the work of a ngag pa to me, scoffing at his neighbors' whisperings of a wandering spirit and saying that, frankly, he did not believe in such superstitious practices. A few days later his own son lay weak from two weeks of illness, unable to eat solid food. He fed the child liquid glucose to build up his strength, and he gave him penicillin to fight off the disease. At the same time, he paid for prayers to be read at Thupten Choling by Tushig Rinpoche. Finally, he called the ngag pa because his wife and father-in-law, who had been out of Chialsa only once, had insisted. When it was his own child who was dying he realized that the stakes were too high to risk a confrontation between a modern education and a traditional background. Only in a crisis did he realize that his balance between the two worlds had left him estranged from both.

Older Tibetans and young Tibetans raised in remote areas seek out the traditional cures without question. For those in a homogeneous Tibetan community such activities come naturally and spontaneously. On religious holidays these refugees visit monasteries, circle stupas, and read scriptures because that is what Tibetan Buddhists have always done. The spiritual world continues to be the most important component in their lives. Younger Tibetans, on the other hand, familiar with the technology of the '80s, choose to celebrate religious holidays by seeing a Hindi video. Like the teacher in Chialsa, they question the value of calling on more traditional sources of assistance. They have lost what Ricouer (quoted in Nowak 1984:2) describes as the "naivete of the first certainty":

> A tradition raises no philosophical problem as long as we live and dwell within it in the naivete of the first certainty. Tradition only becomes problematic when this first naivete is lost. Then we have to retrieve its meaning through and beyond estrangement.

Looked upon by Tibetan leaders as the "seeds of a future Tibet," refugee children struggle to balance the pressures and opportunities of the modern world with their responsibilities to their compatriots and to their nation. ©Peter Forbes

The meaning of ceremonies that had once been inseparable from the ceremony itself is displaced; the Tibetans have lost the purity of the connection with the sacred.

The Dalai Lama fully comprehends the difficulty that Tibetan exiles, children in particular, face in stepping into the twentieth century. They are "young adults who perceive themselves as Tibetans without a country, caught between a traditional world they tend to idealize and a modern future they cannot ignore" (Nowak 1984:63). He recognizes the critical role the generation of children raised as refugees will play in determining the course of the Tibetan nation and culture. These children are looked upon as the "seeds of a future Tibet"; they are the "bearers and defenders of traditional culture and national identity" (Gombo 1975:254).

> We cannot wage war against China; nor can we seriously ask another country to become actively involved in our struggle. What we can do is try to make a name for ourselves by emerging out of our shell and taking part to help the entire world, not just ourselves. Once our people have established themselves as valuable members of the world community, no amount of force can prevent

us from being recognized as a separate race and the rightful owners of our homeland. (*Tibetan Bulletin* 1985:5)

Their parents have provided a foundation in exile; the responsibility for stepping out into the modern world is on the shoulders of these children, the second and the third generations of Tibetans in exile.

The Dalai Lama has served as a guide for these refugees as they try to contend with the inevitable evolution that they and their culture must undergo in order to survive in the twentieth century as Tibetans. In exile he has not remained cloistered in the hills of India, focusing on his spiritual training or on tossing verbal attacks at the Chinese. Rather, he has traveled to the Western world to answer questions concerning Tibetan Buddhism and the Tibetan experience. He has confronted international dilemmas such as nuclear energy and world peace, and examined them from within the context of Tibetan religion. Treated with the respect and ceremony due a world religious leader and an Asian king, he continues to uphold the values of a Tibetan monk. His life proves that the important qualities of Tibetan culture as it existed on the Tibetan plateau continue to hold true in the world of technology. The Dalai Lama has entered the modern world as a refugee; more significantly, he has done so as a Tibetan. He does not ask Tibetans to do anything he has not already done himself.

Chapter 9

The Third Generation

> If one has an education, then by reading books on Tibetan history and religion, he can learn more about our culture; he will see how precious it is and then he will see how important it is to preserve.
> — *Tsering Dhundup, principal of Atisha Primary School, Jawalakhel*

> It was important to set up day schools because we did not want to have generations of carpet weavers.
> — *Wangchuck Tsering, former manager, Himalayan Carpet Exporters*

Jawalakhel, 1985: Every Sunday through Friday at eight in the morning, the school helper solemnly strikes a metal rod against a weighty iron disk to ring the bell of the Atisha Primary School in Jawalakhel. At the sound of the bell, students playing marbles around the small stupa in front of the handicraft center abruptly stop their games and head toward the school. Others come running out from the cluster of brick settlement houses, quickly stuffing leftover bread from home, cucumber slices sprinkled with red chili, or one-rupee candies into their mouths before teachers can confiscate the food. On regular school days the children come dressed in their older, shabbier uniforms: faded gray skirts or pants hitched up over their stomachs and fastened with safety pins, their once-white shirts untucked and buttonless. Over their shoulders, their worn woven bookbags, with TIBET embroidered across the side in faded colors, bulge with paperback textbooks. They enter through the freshly painted, kelly-green gate, cross the small, dusty playing area, and climb the steps to the newly built, two-story white school building. They run to drop off

Much of the children's free time is passed playing games in front of the settlement stupa. In addition to attending school, many also weave carpets at home and help out with the daily chores. ©Peter Forbes

book bags in their respective homerooms and then shove their way into the third-grade classroom for morning prayers.

Lobsang, thin and pale, with thick black glasses dominating his face, stands in front of the classroom. Prayer book in one hand and stick — both for keeping time and for reprimanding wayward students — in the other, Lobsang leads the children through their daily prayers. Every morning in every Tibetan school throughout India and Nepal, Tibetan children chant prayers from a Tibetan text printed in India. These prayers, sung in the high-pitched voices of young boys and girls, lack the haunting, hypnotic quality of the scriptures chanted by older monks; yet even the sing-song quality of these mechanically read prayers has a power and beauty of its own.

Prayers over, the students rush outside to skip rope, play marbles, or visit the bathroom, three or four children pushing their way into a stall at once.

The teachers begin to wander toward the second-floor room that, during the course of the 1985 school year, gradually came to look like a real school office. Construction on the school building had been completed the week

Cultural Survival 103

before the school was officially opened at a ceremony on an auspicious day in March 1985. While community leaders spoke on the importance of education, the "fat" lama of the settlement chanted prayers, clanged cymbals, and pounded his drum in the office to pray for the school's future success.

Earlier in the year, the office was an empty classroom with one desk surrounded by piles and piles of dusty Tibetan textbooks, English textbooks donated by the International School in Kathmandu, English storybooks, French game books, and Nepalese textbooks. There were no class schedules, no school rules or guidelines, no blackboard erasers, no paper, and few records from the previous school year.

Five months later, a long table with a small drawer for each teacher occupies the center of the office; two bookshelves stand against the wall filled with dusted books arranged according to subject. There is even a cabinet filled with files of tests and report cards, and a class schedule is drawn in colored chalk on the blackboard.

The slow and relatively steady improvement in the school since its establishment is most visible in the morning assemblies. Every morning at 8:45, after the short break following prayers, the bell rings for assembly. During the first few months, this assembly was pitiful: dirty children in dirty clothes forced into crooked lines by bored teachers, mindlessly singing the Tibetan and Nepalese national anthems, inevitably off-key and off-beat. After completing these songs, the students raced into their classroom and the teachers slowly straggled off for another day of class.

The construction of a new school brought new teachers, new energy, and new ideas. Six months into the school year, the school staged a dramatic production with skits in Nepali, Tibetan, and English. Every evening the students willingly returned to school to practice songs for *Snow White* and to learn the steps to Tibetan dances. They helped build a stage and they gladly assisted in the cleanup. Later the school sponsored a fair to raise money for extracurricular activities. Finally, in the fall of 1985, the First Annual Inter-Tibetan School Competition was held in Kathmandu. Modeled after the annual competitions held among the Tibetan central schools in India, this competition included athletic events, a marching contest, and academic quizzes.

When compared with the standard of similar events held in the Tibetan schools in India, the competition may not have seemed that impressive. Given the history of education in Nepal and the difficulties and setbacks encountered by the Education Ministry in Dharmsala, however, the event seemed to mark an important turning point for Tibetan education in this country. The competition served to spark the excitement and interest of students, parents, and teachers in education and in extracurricular activities, and it reaffirmed the government-in-exile's commitment to improving the quality of Tibetan education in Nepal. Most important, the event gave Tibetans the hope that the black years for education in Nepal were over.

*   *   *   *   *

> The Tibetans in general have come to view and consider education as an importance of top national interest. By and large, one would not be too far wrong to say that the Tibetans consider education not just an instrument for the preservation of their identity but also as a tool with which it gain their ultimate goal — independence. (Rapstong 1985:3)

Even before leaving Tibet, the Dalai Lama recognized that providing his people with a modern education was essential not only for their own well being but also for the survival of Tibetan culture in the twentieth century. In exile, education became even more important; Tibetan leaders saw it as the key to raising children who were both proud of their cultural heritage and also equipped to contribute meaningfully to their own community and to the society in which they were living (Rapstong1985:3).

"We are now in India and we must work to perpetuate those beliefs for which we had to give up our country," the Dalai Lama says.

> In order to promote our national struggle, therefore, we must evolve a long-term effort to preserve and further our faith and culture. Towards this end we have set up special schools for our children and have sent Tibetan teachers wherever we have Tibetans abroad, so they may become good Tibetans and help to carry out the political and moral struggle. (Dalai Lama 1969:191)

"Our primary aim is to go back to Tibet and to get back our country," says Rinchen Dharlo. "Then we will need engineers, doctors, teachers, and scientists." Indian schools would not do. The Dalai Lama immediately began to establish independent schools where Tibetan subjects could be included with a modern curriculum and where the Ministry of Education, a branch of the government-in-exile created shortly after arriving in India, could ensure that the standard of the teachers and the education provided was satisfactory.

Because of communication difficulties with India, it was some time before the refugees in Nepal heard of and were included in the Dalai Lama's plans. Once again, foreigners living in Nepal — those on Father Moran's committee in particular — became the driving force behind creating schools and convincing the refugees to send their children there. Motivated by a sense of urgency that the Tibetan culture was in danger of dying out, members of Father Moran's committee met in July 1961 to discuss plans for separate Tibetan schools. "If we feel that Tibetans have a contribution to make to world society," the minutes read, "then we should make every effort to help them make it."

Shortly after the Jawalakhel crafts center opened in 1961, this committee set up a small day school in a bamboo hut with funds from ICRC. The children, who had been collecting water and digging holes for the past year, were now sent to the mud-floored school.

The Dalai Lama and other educated Tibetans were aware of the value of education; for the majority of Tibetans, however, sending their children to school was simply a matter of economics. Few families were willing to give up the extra income their children could bring in from weaving carpets in exchange for the intangible benefits of an education. An an incentive, the first schools were free and included free lunches. Even though Karma, the young boy who had traveled down from Jomson with his parents, was old enough to work and earn money, his parents sent him to school just so he could get a free meal.

Because the Tibetans had not yet made contact with the newly formed Education Ministry in Dharmsala, the curriculum and organization of the school was left to Father Moran's committee. Certain components of this responsibility created problems. Members of the committee disagreed amongst themselves and with the Tibetans about how much English to teach the refugees. Father Moran recalls:

> "First you have to learn Nepali," I explained to the Tibetans. "If you are fluent in English and Tibetan but a fool in Nepali you'll get cheated on the streets. If you have no Nepalese friends who can help you? Whose advice can you get to start a business or a store?" People at that level of society didn't need English. They needed Nepali.

One Christian member of the committee argued that instead of instruction in Buddhism, these children should be learning about Easter and Christmas. "They weren't ready for that," Father Moran said.

> I told them, "Let those children know what they were supposed to be. Then if they're not satisfied we can teach them Christianity. It's more important for them to have a good conscience; a good Buddhist is better than a bad Christian." That surprised them. At first they thought we were a mission enterprise. The committee was for the Tibetan people and we weren't out to destroy the good things in their culture.

The foreigners tried to promote Tibetan Buddhism, Tibetan language, and Tibetan handicrafts. They established a night school where teenagers working in the factory during the day could study the Tibetan and Nepali language. Every evening, all the children and teenagers in the settlement learned Tibetan dances. "They were learning the high culture of Lhasa in a refugee school in Nepal!" Father Moran exclaimed. Local Tibetans who had received some formal education in India or Kalimpong volunteered to teach whatever English, Tibetan, or mathematics they knew to the first class of 25 students. Father Moran hired Tibetan monks to teach Tibetan subjects in the school. A local Nepalese taught Nepali, and Peace Corps workers, volunteers for the Dooley Foundation, and other foreigners living in Kathmandu came to teach English. "The children were very interested in learning," one of the first teachers recalls. "They liked to carry their books very much." They studied Tibetan language and history from Tibetan texts printed by the government-in-exile; learned Nepali from books purchased by Father Moran's committee; English, math, and science were taught from texts donated by the international community in Nepal. Blackboards, benches, and desks were built by the refugees, and teachers' salaries were paid by Father Moran's committee.

Because few children had had any previous education, all ages gathered in the one-room hut. Because Karma was one of the oldest, he was often left in charge when teachers went out of the classroom. He would stand in front with a stick leading the children through recitations of lines of poetry written on the board in Tibetan or Nepali by a teacher—lines that Karma still recalls today. Everyone quickly grew bored with this exercise, however, and bedlam broke out, forcing the teacher to return to his job.

Foreign volunteers took the children on field trips to look at magazines and picture books at the American library; others went to the Marine House, where the students ate hamburgers and drank Coca Cola while the volunteer visited her boyfriend. Father Moran arranged for the Tibetan children to walk to St. Xavier's, the Jesuit boarding school of which he was founder and principal, for their free lunches. During these lunches, Nepalese students taught the refugees proper table manners.

Twenty-three years later, Tenzin, the son of one of these first Tibetan students, accompanied me on one of my daily visits to St. Xavier's to collect my mail. We went through a back door and walked into the library, where we were greeted by Father Moran. The white-haired priest, wearing his flowing, black cape and a small, black beret, knelt down to speak with Tenzin, asking him slowly in Nepali if he would like some bread and butter. Tenzin's eyes grew wide, his skin paled, and this four-year-old boy who only moments before had eaten a handful of cookies and proudly announced that his stomach was not sick tugged me toward the door, shrieking in Tibetan that his stomach was not well, that his stomach was very sick, that it was time to go home. Smiling, Father Moran followed us down the narrow hallway and offered the child a handful of Indian candy. Eyes flooded with tears, Tenzin accepted the candy and cried for me to hurry, that we had to go home. As we stepped back into the chaos of the Nepali street, Tenzin still clutching my hand, I wondered what his thoughts had been, and as we walked along I tried to imagine his father's first images of this gruff-looking priest.

Despite the foreigners' efforts to create good schools in Nepal, most refugee families with school-age children continued their exodus south to India where, they had heard, they could enroll their children in the Tibetan schools opened by the Dalai Lama. "Jawalakhel was more like a transit camp," Karma recalls. "People would arrive, stay a few months, and move on; the population was always changing." As a boy of 13, Karma wanted desperately to join his peers for schooling in India. His father returned to the lama in Boudha and asked for advice regarding his son's education. The lama read the mo and recommended that Karma remain in Nepal. Karma was disappointed and angry; every day more of his friends left, and soon he was the only child over 10 in the school. For years, he says, he was so bitter that he refused to visit that same lama. Now, after 25 years, he realizes that he has had a good life in Nepal and that in fact the lama had given him the best possible advice.

In 1965, the Norwegian Refugee Council contributed funds to replace the dark, dilapidated hut with a new, brick schoolhouse. By this time, the Swiss had assumed complete responsibility for the carpet factories and the refugees were beginning to stand on their own feet. Their job more or less complete, Father Moran's committee handed responsibility for the schools in Jawalakhel, Chialsa, Tashi Palkhiel, and Dhorpatan over to SATA and then disbanded.

The Swiss immediately established an office to oversee Tibetan education and hired an education specialist to recruit teachers from the different Tibetan settlements. SATA held month-long training courses for all teachers in the Carpet Trading Company's building in Jawalakhel. These workshops were meant to "convey the practical and methodological way of teaching the subjects of the Nepalese syllabus for primary schools to the teachers." During one afternoon session in the summer of 1965, a teacher from Tashi Palkhiel was teaching a lesson in astronomy. Pointing to a map of the universe, he explained that the earth was round and that it revolved around the sun. An older monk stood up and yelled at the younger teacher for telling such lies. "Are you a Tibetan? You're not a Tibetan! Are you a Buddhist? You're not a Buddhist! How can you think you are and still say that the world is round! The world is flat!" he cried. Everyone in the class burst out laughing, and the Swiss instructor motioned for the young teacher to ignore the attack and proceed with his lesson.

In 1973 SATA's education office handed its responsibilities over to the newly formed Snow Lion Foundation. Having just completed a training program himself, Karma, as secretary of the foundation, suddenly found himself responsible for everything from paying teachers' salaries to

This Rinpoche was in the first group of refugees trained as teachers by SATA. He continued teaching Tibetan in the Mount Everest School in Chialsa until his death in 1988. ©Ann Forbes

appointing principals, selecting texts, and repairing school benches. Before he had much of a chance to master his new duties, however, the Nepal government exerted control and changed the picture for education in Nepal.

The standard of the Tibetan schools in Nepal has never equaled that of the boarding schools established by the Dalai Lama in India. By the late 1960s, however, the Tibetan day schools were far superior to the Nepalese schools that had opened around the country. During this period, Nepalese leaders began to recognize the essential role that education played in modernization and in creating a Nepalese national identity. In 1971 the government instituted a five-year plan that set a minimum standard of education to be available to all children in Nepal. Known as the New Education Plan, it called for the nationalization of existing private schools and the implementation of Nepali as the language of instruction. In February 1974, the Nepalese government forced the Tibetan community to hand over the administration and ownership of all their schools in Nepal.

Under the plan, Nepalese students had to be admitted into the all-Tibetan schools. Since only Nepalese citizens could legally teach in the government schools, Tibetan teachers, who were not yet allowed to become Nepalese citizens, were forbidden to teach during regular school hours. Tibetan language, history, and religion were erased from the school curriculum, and no language other than Nepali could be taught during school hours. Because the Tibetan leaders felt that instruction in Tibetan subjects and in English was essential to the children's education, they asked the Tibetan teachers to offer Tibetan and English classes before and after school. The additional class time ensured that the students would not fall too far behind in these subjects and also provided the Tibetan teachers with part-time employment. The longer hours, however, forced six- to thirteen-year-olds to be in school every day from 7:30 in the morning until 8:00 at night.

The New Education Plan took all administrative control away from Tibetan teachers and the Snow Lion Foundation; they were forced to stand by helplessly as the academic standards of their students and their schools degenerated. Many Tibetans chose to teach because they felt that they were playing an important role in affecting the future of their culture and their country. "Teachers," explains the Dalai Lama, "should help children be not only able to earn a living later but also to appreciate their identity as a Tibetan and to contribute to our cause" (Dalai Lama 1985:3). Teachers also often believed that working for the Tibetan community was the most effective means of repaying the government for their own education. After the New Education Plan was introduced, many of the more motivated and ambitious teachers quickly became frustrated and left to seek more fulfilling jobs elsewhere. The overall quality of the teachers declined dramatically and Karma found it almost impossible to find replacements.

To meet its operating expenses, the Nepalese administration had to charge admission fees. Although the refugees were no longer starving, the majority of the Tibetans in the Jawalakhel settlement could not possibly afford the minimal fee; even if they could, many parents were still only willing to send their children to school if it was free. In order to keep Tibetans in school, the Snow Lion Foundation had to bear the cost of school fees for all of the Tibetan students. Since these fees did not cover any one-time costs such as building renovations or new additions, the parents and

Nationalized in 1974, Tibetan schools in Nepal are believed to offer a lower quality education than that available in the schools in India. Since 1982, the Tibetan community has resumed control of many of those schools and improvements are slowly being made. This school in Dhorpatan is one of the last to receive attention.
©Ann Forbes

the Nepalese principals also asked the foundation to contribute money to make necessary improvements.

Karma was caught in a bind: it was his responsibility to enhance the quality of education available to Tibetan children. After providing the money, however, he was then unable to oversee the upkeep and management of the changes; a short while after completing one project, he would be called on to provide funds for another. For example, time and time again the Snow Lion Foundation sent money to Chialsa to repair windows broken by local Sherpa students whom the teachers could not control. Almost immediately after the repairs were completed, Karma would receive a message from Chialsa that the windows in another classroom had been broken and that the room could not be used until the foundation could meet the costs of replacement.

In 1977 and 1978, the Norwegian Refugee Council funded the construction of an addition to the school in Jawalakhel so that it could offer the sixth and seventh grades. Once the construction was complete, the

Nepal government claimed that since the school now had vacancies, it must be merged with a nearby Nepalese high school. The school, which had been 95 percent Tibetan, now became 10 percent Tibetan and 90 percent Nepalese; the Tibetan children became a minority in a school financed primarily by their own community.

Conditions at the school in Jawalakhel continued to deteriorate. Since classes were dull and teachers negligent, the Tibetan students began to show up at school for roll call and then leave to roam the streets. When tourist buses arrived at the carpet factory, the children surrounded them, begging for money and candy and handing out their addresses with pleas for second-hand clothing. Many of the students who were older than 14 left school to weave carpets in the factory or to join monasteries. Of those who joined monasteries, many soon dropped out and returned to hang out in the streets.

Tibetan parents and teachers complained to the camp management and to Dhundup Namgyal, the Tibetan welfare officer, about the condition of the school. Mr. Namgyal repeatedly pleaded with the Nepal government ministers and secretaries, asking for Tibetan language to be included in the curriculum and for the Tibetan government-in-exile to be allowed to resume control of its schools. The government officials dismissed his requests, saying, "Now you are living in Nepal and you do not need any Tibetan knowledge. If your children get Nepalese studies, that is enough." Other officials explained that there were many different dialects and cultural groups in Nepal. If Tibetans, whom the Nepalese now considered to be a permanent fixture in their country, were allowed to study their own language, then all the other groups would request the same treatment. If each ethnic group spoke its own language, Nepal would have no national language, no national culture, and thus no national identity.

School conditions throughout Nepal were similar to those of Jawalakhel. Teachers would take turns coming to school; when they did come, they would write a few lessons on the board and then go sit outside to pass the time. In 1981 the Nepal government, finally acknowledging that the nationalization of the schools had been a failure, passed the Seventh Amendment Education Rules allowing private schools to reopen. The Tibetans now had a chance to regain control of their schools.

By this time, however, 1,000 students were enrolled in the original Tibetan school in Jawalakhel and 29 teachers were employed by the Nepalese government. In 1974, when the school had been nationalized, there had been 100 students and Karma had paid the salaries for seven teachers. The Snow Lion Foundation had neither the staff nor the money to resume administrative and financial responsibility for the school, and it did not have nearly enough funds to start a separate one.

Nepali class in the Dhorpatan school. ©Ann Forbes

Two years later, in 1983, a government-in-exile officer from Dharmsala on an official tour of the settlements in Nepal visited the handicraft center in Jawalakhel. He was shocked to see so many Tibetan children wandering the streets during school hours, and he asked why they were not in classes. After hearing the dismal history of the Jawalakhel school, he insisted that something be done immediately. Several months later, a vacant Nepalese home was rented in Jawalakhel to serve as a temporary Tibetan school. Karma eventually obtained financial assistance from MISEROR, a German international relief organization, to construct a primary school on a small plot of land behind the carpet factory. In 1985 the Atisha Primary School, named after a famous and revered religious teacher in India who had visited Tibet in 1042 to teach the Buddhist doctrine, was opened in the new building in Jawalakhel.

*   *   *   *   *

While Karma was working to find a solution in Jawalakhel, he was also seeking ways to regain control of the Tibetan schools in the other camps. By 1986, when the Chialsa school was officialy signed back over to the refugees, the Snow Lion Foundation was once again in charge of seven of the twelve refugee schools in Nepal. Having overcome this major hurdle, Karma continues to face the problems of limited funding and scarce resources that exist in all of the Tibetan schools, in India and in Nepal.

Tsering Dhundup, who has a master's degree in education from Chandigar University, became the principal of the Atisha Primary School in 1986. He lives in a tiny, cement-block room in the run-down brick building that had once housed the Swiss poultry farm in the 1960s. The doors of 10 other similar rooms—each housing families of four, five, and six—open out onto a flat, stone courtyard. In the center is a single water spigot where everyone in the building gets water, washes dishes and clothing, and bathes. Children begin crying at five o'clock in the morning, often to the sounds of the drunk living upstairs who beats his wife regularly. Because there is no latrine, the residents relieve themselves in the ditch by the side of the road. Tsering lives in this building because it is almost impossible to find an affordable room in a nicer area on his 900-rupee (US$38) monthly salary.

If he were a teacher in India, he would receive room and board in addition to his salary; the Snow Lion Foundation cannot afford to offer these benefits to its employees. More significantly, while Tsering would not earn much more money by teaching in a Tibetan school in India, his salary at least would be comparable to, if not slightly higher than, the average salary of the refugee population in that country. In Nepal, however, where owning a private business can be so lucrative, Tsering is significantly poorer than many educated men his age. He was once offered a job doing the accounts in a private carpet factory where he could have earned much more money and, he feels, the respect of the young entrepreneurs. He did not accept the job, however, because he says that "a teacher is the torch bearer of the nation; they shape the child from the beginning." Last year Tsering married and he and his wife recently had a child, responsibilities that will only intensify the financial pressures that his idealism must withstand. The scarcity of bright, qualified teachers is particularly prevalent in Nepal, and is a constant source of concern for Karma.

The financial pressures hindering the quality of the schools are countered by the refugees' growing appreciation for the importance of education. A 50-year-old Tibetan women who has not left Chialsa since her arrival 20 years ago laments her children's poor academic performance and lack of interest in their studies. If they had studied hard and done well in school, she said, she would have done all the chores willingly. Instead of doing homework, however, her daughters slept, daydreamed, and played. They eventually quit school and were put to work in the carpet factory to earn their keep. "Yes, they are helpful with the work at home," their mother said. "But when they grow up, it isn't good or worthwhile. If they knew their studies, their lives would be okay, but if they just weave, their life is empty. We're all fools."

"In carpet business," one carpet shop owner explained, "you worry all the time and there's no peace. But if you earn enough money to give your children a good education, later you don't have to worry if you can't give them money; they can stand on their own feet." "Twenty-five years later it has come to a point where there are so many people even willing to pay fees for school that there is a long application list at the central schools in India," Tenzin Geyche, the Dalai Lama's personal secretary, observes. "The Tibetans are really intent on giving their children the best type of education they can afford."

For Tibetans, the ideal education would offer a strong curriculum with a balance of Tibetan and modern subjects. It is difficult and expensive to acquire the staff and the resources necessary to provide such high quality instruction, and often the Tibetan schools fall short of the standards set by their leaders and by a growing proportion of the population.

Many Tibetans who can afford to pay the monthly fees of US$70-100, compared to the $2-5 charges in Tibetan schools, are sending their children to the private "English medium" boarding academies established during England's rule in India. The academic standard of these schools is far superior to any of the Tibetan primary schools in Nepal or even the Tibetan central schools in India. Students become quite proficient in English and they obtain a solid foundation in mathematics, science, and history. In exchange, however, they often speak English more readily than Tibetan, they have difficulties writing Tibetan, and they know little about the history of Tibet. "Because I went to an 'English medium' school," a 25-year-old carpet exporter said, "it's very difficult for me to know Tibetan language and culture. For learning Tibetan culture the school makes a big difference."

Although most Tibetan schools are English medium and offer science, math, and history, their greatest strength is the fact that they are Tibetan. Every schoolbook printed by the Tibetan press in India includes a brief statement about the flight from Tibet. When students are asked to write an essay, the topic is either the Dalai Lama or the Chinese invasion; when a Tibetan leader visits the school, he always introduces or concludes his remarks by saying, "We are not in our own country, we are in exile. We have not a piece of land, not even the space of our hand, so we are living on someone else's land. Our land is Tibet and whatever you do, it should be towards gaining our independence."

Every morning in every Tibetan school in exile, students are led through prayers for the long life of the Dalai Lama and for the happiness of all sentient beings. Here students in Chialsa gather in one classroom for their daily prayers. ©Ann Forbes

After Karma's friend offered to send his daughter to an English boarding school in India, Karma was suddenly forced to consider the implications that such a move would have on his daughter and, indirectly, on the Tibetan community as a whole. He explained:

> One side of me really wants her to do something professional. If she could do well in school, I would be willing to send her to an English school at the price of her Tibetan-ness. But then, the other side is afraid that she won't do anything. If she could not become something professional, then it is much better for her to learn Tibetan culture and traditions. All religions are good but as I am a Buddhist, I want my children to be the same. If she goes to a Tibetan school she will learn all the basic ideas of Buddhism. She will be raised in the religion so she doesn't need to go to any effort to learn about it. If she lost her Tibetan-ness and is only okay in her studies, I will be very sad. A Tibetan who doesn't know Tibetan is like a bird with only one wing.

Karma ultimately chose a Tibetan school over the English medium school, as did the manager of Jawalakhel for his son. Having worked for the government-in-exile, these men are conscious of the significance of their choice for the future of their country. Their decision, however, seems to be becoming the exception rather than the rule.

*   *   *   *   *

As the refugees become more integrated into the modern world and as they are exposed to the opportunities of that world, they are raising their expectations. Constrained by limited resources, the government-in-exile is not always able to fulfill the expectations, especially when they pertain to education. Increasingly parents are being forced to choose between sending their children to a school that will provide them with the skills necessary to be successful in twentieth-century society or one that will give them an understanding and appreciation for their own cultural heritage. It is a tradeoff the Tibetans had hoped to avoid. Moreover, the implications of this choice are ones they are reluctant to see as very significant. A child does not need to read the language or know the order of the Tibetan kings, they say, to be committed to the Tibetan cause. Thus far, their conclusion seems to be accurate. Only the future can tell us if the third generation's commitment to their cause is dependent upon embracing Tibetan history, language, and religion.

Chapter 10

The Community

> I think exposure to other cultures, other ways of life is bound to influence an individual's interest in Tibetan studies in some way. Whether a person is influenced or can withstand that influence depends on how well we can retain our traditional values. In that regard, even as a Tibetan, I am surprised when I see young Tibetans who have gone through a modern education sincerely devoted to their religious practices. Even though they are involved in business, they go out and enjoy, go to movies, to discotheques, but still they retain many of their Tibetan traditions. I see them saying their daily prayers, being polite, humble and compassionate, and remaining loyal to the Dalai Lama.
>
> — *Tenzin Geyche, personal secretary to the Dalai Lama*

Yeshi, an engaging, 26-year-old Tibetan woman with a master's degree in education, teaches science at the Tibetan School in Boudha. A foreign sponsor sent Yeshi to a missionary school when she was a young girl, and she later graduated from Chandigar University in the Punjab. She wears t-shirts and blue jeans, jokes and argues with her boyfriend, and likes Bruce Springsteen. She speaks flawless English, is informed about events in Central America, South Africa, and the United States, and likes foreign films.

Yeshi moved to Nepal from India because her mother wanted to be near the sacred stupas at Boudha and Swayambhunath. Yeshi feels strongly that Tibetans, particularly those who are educated, should work for the government-in-exile, so she worked as a secretary for Himalayan Carpet Exporters for a year, even though she was bored. When she is sick she takes Tibetan medicine; every night she circles the Bodnath stupa, and on holidays she and her boyfriend make pilgrimages to the holy sites in the Kathmandu area.

I accompanied Tashi, her boyfriend, and Yeshi to Namu Buddha, a shrine set on top of a hill on the eastern outskirts of the Kathmandu valley. In a previous lifetime, the Buddha had come across a tigress who could find no food to feed her cubs. To prevent their starving, the tigress was preparing to kill herself so they would have meat to eat. Moved by compassion, the Buddha cut his own hand so the animals would smell his blood, and sacrificed his own body so the mother could survive to watch over her cubs. A shrine and a stupa were later built to commemorate this act.

On the day of the full moon in July, the three of us boarded a rickety bus in Kathmandu and headed out across the lush rice fields of the monsoon season to a village near the Buddhist site. Upon arriving at the village, we climbed up the worn path through a misty drizzle to the spot of the Buddha's sacrifice. Tashi and Yeshi prostrated before the stone shrine, placed an offering at the base, and requested that a certain prayer be read by monks in the small, whitewashed monastery nearby. That evening, as the full moon edged over the hills, they circled the stupa, kneading their prayer beads and casually chatting with other worshippers. The following morning they chanted "Om Mani Padme Hum" over and over as we walked the four hours back to the bus.

The first time I met Yeshi, at a Lohsar celebration a week after my arrival, she praised the Dalai Lama and stressed that I must do whatever I could to meet him. Yeshi's education contributes to her appreciation of her culture and religion; yet a deep sense of pride in being Tibetan and having the Dalai Lama as a leader is just as evident among those who have received little formal education. The Dalai Lama tells the Tibetans that, though important, an education is not enough; he says that children must also be able to "respect human values, to be sincere, honest and compassionate." These values are not something that can be taught in school; one learns them by experience, by living in a family that lives by these and other "Tibetan" values, and by growing up in a community that is proud of this cultural heritage.

Yeshi was a boarding student at a missionary school where Christian prayers were read daily, but she spent her vacations with her family in a refugee settlement. "At the moment the Tibetan identity is still intact," Rinchen Dharlo, former representative of the Dalai Lama in Nepal, now representative in New York, comments. "The children do not have to study it purposely, they learn it naturally. They spend almost 24 hours within the Tibetan community. . . . If Tibetans had lived separately, however, by this time they would have lost their culture."

Located on a major trekking route on the outskirts of Pokhara, Tashi Palkhiel is one of the most vibrant refugee settlements in Nepal. ©Ann Forbes

*   *   *   *   *

From the dirt road leading northeast out of Pokhara, the blue, green, and yellow prayer flags of Tashi Palkhiel can be spotted. On a clear day the snow-covered peaks of the Annapurna Range stretch across the horizon, the majestic pinnacle of Machapuchare, the Fish Tail, jutting into the sky. Trekkers on their way to these mountains walk or ride in jeeps up through the flat valley of the Kali Gandaki River, passing tiny thatched tea huts and mud houses scattered alongside the road. Corn and wheat grow in the fertile, flat fields next to the river, and stone walls convenient for resting are scattered under the shade of an occasional banana or mango tree.

Tashi Palkhiel, a 45-minute walk from Pokhara, is nestled on a shelf between the river and a cliff rising sharply to a plateau of cornfields. Small tea stalls and souvenir shops line the road near the settlement. Teenage Tibetan boys wearing Michael Jackson t-shirts with turned-up jacket collars hang around playing *Pok*, a Chinese gambling game. Rock or Hindi music blares from a tape deck nearby. Brightly painted signs in English and Tibetan beckon trekkers to come see a typical Tibetan refugee settlement, and older Tibetans dressed in chubbas and rainbow-colored aprons cry out to foreign passersby to buy their jewelry and other "antique" Tibetan handicrafts.

Inside the settlement, dirt paths wind around whitewashed mud and stone houses. Stone walls topped with red-blossomed cacti surround the clusters of houses and keep the donkeys, cows, and water buffalo that run freely in the valley away from the homes. The older, thatched-roof buildings are slowly being replaced by less picturesque, but watertight, cement houses with tin roofs. Communal water faucets are found at junctures in the path; women sit in clusters under trees spinning wool, drinking tea, and nursing babies. Bright yellow, green, and blue prayer flags, new from the recent Lohsar celebrations, fly overhead.

The handicraft center lies on the northern edge of the settlement. The wooden cathedral ceiling of the office building reflects the influence of its Swiss architect and contrasts strikingly with the one-story Nepalese-style weaving hall and storage room. On weekdays, the grassy area enclosed by the stone buildings bustles with activity. Trucks drive up to dump off shipments of raw wool from Tibet, and middle-aged men and women spread freshly dyed wool in the sun to dry. Several workers weigh a completed order of carpets and load them onto the trucks bound for Kathmandu; the sound of pounding hammers and singing girls rises out of the weaving hall.

A dispensary is housed in an empty office in the handicraft center. Although the Swiss opened small clinics in each of their camps, many of these clinics have since closed because of insufficient funding. Where they do continue, they are often managed by untrained workers handing out medicine that has passed its expiration date. In the early 1980s, the Norwegian Refugee Council introduced a health project to train community health workers and to upgrade the clinic. Gradually, over the course of three years, the Norwegians reduced their financial and managerial involvement so that the Tibetans could learn how to maintain the clinics and provide adequate health care to the community. Paljorling, a camp in the center of Pokhara, and Tashi Ling, on the southeastern edge, are also included in this health project. A similar program was recently initiated in Kathmandu under the auspices of the Tibetan government-in-exile with assistance from foreign agencies.

Behind the handicraft center is the Mount Kailesh school, opened by Father Moran's committee in 1963 with two grades and 180 students. The Jesuit would visit the school regularly, bringing old Christmas cards, pictures, and magazines to distribute as prizes and gifts. He taught the children phrases from songs, new games, and English words.

The Tibetan day school was nationalized in 1974 and opened to local

Nepalese children. Since only a handful of Nepalese joined the school, it remained a manageable size and was the first Tibetan school to become private after the Seventh Amendment Education Rules were instituted in 1981. The Snow Lion Foundation immediately switched the school from Nepali back to English medium; gave a placement test, which put most students back several grades; and reopened the school. In 1986 it had six grades, 117 students, and seven teachers; classes had recently moved into six new cement classrooms built with funds from the Norwegian Refugee Council and from private donors. This school has had a particularly large number of foreign teachers; when a Westerner walks into a class, the children promptly stand up and say, politely, "Good Morning Miss (Sir)" before bursting into song. (Born and bred in West Virginia, I was a bit surprised by their choice of the song "Almost Heaven, West Virginia" on the day I visited the school!)

The parents in Tashi Palkhiel are proud of the improvements in their school. Until recently, those who could afford the school fees enrolled their children in the superior Tibetan central schools in India. Now, Tsering, the production manager of the carpet factory, an articulate, middle-aged mother of two, said the refugees no longer think it is necessary to send children away to get a good education.

The voices rising from the upper grades of the school are conspicuously female. The sixth grade has thirteen girls and only one boy; the missing boys can be found just next door, in the village monastery. The monastery, which sports fresh coats of red, orange, and white paint, is enclosed by a high stone wall with chips of glass embedded in the top (for keeping out intruders or keeping in potential escapees?). Young boys are everywhere. In two years, 40 monks have joined the monastery. There is a Tibetan saying, the manager of the settlement explained: "What was once a lot of flames [Buddhism] is now no more, only the ashes and coals remain." Tibetan parents feel very strongly about rekindling the flame of religion in exile, he said, and so they send their young boys off to become monks.

As in Tibet, this is not the only reason children become monks. Sending a child to a monastery eases the financial burden on a poor family. Some young children are forced into the religious life because it is the most respected profession in the community. It is usually only when children are in their teens that they decide for themselves to become monks or nuns for religious reasons.

The monks live in a hostel in the gonpa, eat in a mess hall, and take classes in Tibetan, English, and Nepali. Most of the four- to sixteen-year-old boys' time, however, is spent memorizing scriptures and praying under the guidance of a senior monk. They have little free time left in which to play and, except on designated days, they are not allowed to leave

Young monks looking through the gate of the monastery to their peers playing in the school yard. ©Ann Forbes

the compound. Because the school is so close, these young monks can easily see and hear the shouts and songs of their peers, who are free to go wherever they please and do whatever they want.

Tsering, the production manager of the carpet factory, thinks these children are being sent to the monastery far too early. "When they are sent so young without any real understanding, they are ready to leave and get married by the time they've grown up." She also feels the monastery is too close to the local community. Ideally, gonpas should be isolated so the monks are able to concentrate on religion without the distractions of the everyday world. Uninhabited land is scarce in Nepal, however, and in Tashi Palkhiel the Tibetans built the monastery on the only available space they had.

Problems arising from the proximity of a monastery to the lay community are not unique to Tashi Palkhiel. The Dalai Lama is concerned that in Boudha in particular, the constant intermingling of monks with the lay population is undermining the "proper discipline and proper decorations" that a monastery must maintain. "There are certain rules and regulations that monks have to follow," he has said, "and in the existing monasteries in Nepal, some are not following these strictly." Tenzin Geyche, his personal secretary, elaborated:

> Many times the monasteries are just there because of tradition or to make money. The monasteries in south India maintain the proper dress and proper discipline; monasteries in Nepal are of the same lineage but the tradition is not proper. Monks roam around, they go to movies. Whenever this happens, it is better for them not to be a monk.

* * * * *

Because the camp is close to Pokhara and is located on the main trekking road into the Annapurna Range, Tibetans have been able to earn additional money selling crafts to tourists. Like the early entrepreneurs of Kathmandu, these refugees pack their goods — jewelry, silver knives and bowls, real antiques from Tibet, and imitations made in Kathmandu — into cheaply made Nepalese knapsacks and cycle to the shore of the lake in Pokhara. These and other Tibetans who sell their wares by the side of the road are called, "something sellers," as a mockery of their pestering cry, "Do you want to buy something? Can I sell you something?" Under the shadow of Machapuchare, these "something sellers" spread their wares on the ground by the lake and call out for the tourists' attention and money. During the prime trekking seasons in Nepal, production in the carpet factory drops off as workers abandon their looms and head to the lakeside. The availability of economic alternatives, however, serves as an incentive to remain in the settlement for those refugees who do not want to live solely on the salary of the carpet factory.

Most of the Tibetans now living in Tashi Palkhiel entered Nepal along a trade route from the village of Jangthang in western Tibet. They spent several years near the village of Jomson, in the Mustang district, before following the advice of ICRC workers and settling on land outside of Pokhara. Under the foreigners' direction, the refugees began clearing an airstrip so food rations could be flown in. Tibetan volunteers carried the rations the 45-minute walk from the airstrip to the settlement, where community representatives appointed by the Swiss distributed them among the refugees. The refugees spun wool brought in by plane into yarn, which was then flown back to the Jawalakhel Handicraft Center; they sold their valuables, and they waited anxiously to go home.

When selecting the representatives in the various settlements, the Swiss sought out those who had been in positions of authority in Tibet and then asked for the refugees' approval of their selection. Karma Gyurmey, who is known as "Chief Karma" to Tibetans, was unanimously elected.

A district leader in Tibet, Chief Karma had tried to continue his work under the Chinese, but because of an "ideological conflict" with the Chinese staff, he eventually decided it was best to leave: "The Chinese were aggressive and were taking our human rights. They said they came to help Tibetans but instead, with power, they oppressed." Karma entered Nepal through Mustang and lived with nomads from Jangthang for a year along the border. In 1963, His Majesty's Government of Nepal ordered the refugees to move further away from the border, offering them seven acres of empty land outside Pokhara on the condition that the Tibetans or their Swiss helpers construct water supply facilities for the neighboring Nepalese village. More than 100 families packed up their white canvas tents, their bed rolls, and their wooden bowls and traveled south for 10 days to set up their new home. SATA, the same organization helping the refugees in Jawalakhel, soon arrived to oversee the construction of houses and to establish a carpet factory. "In the beginning the people faced some problems," Chief Karma recalls, "but not at all like the problems faced by those remaining in Tibet. We learned a new craft under complete freedom, under no oppression, so it was really no problem." When the Swiss handed over the carpet center management in 1966, they designated Chief Karma as manager of the settlement; he has remained in that position ever since.

Tashi Palkhiel has its problems: there is a shortage of land on which to expand; running water is in short supply due to disagreements with Nepalese neighbors; and the day care center is housed in a tiny, bleak, cement-walled room. But unlike many of the refugee settlements in Nepal, Tashi Palkhiel looks and feels like a village – a permanent village. People are working and making money. children are learning, and new houses are being built. Another settlement manager commented that Tashi Palkhiel was "the best-run and the best overall camp in Nepal."

In spite of difficult conditions and changes in the carpet industry over the past 25 years, the carpet factory in Tashi Palkhiel has maintained its reputation for producing a steady supply of good-quality carpets. Tashi Phuntsok, manager of the Carpet Trading Company, says, "This success is all due to the honesty and untiring zeal of the workers and the management of the center. Unfortunately, these qualities are not found in other centers" (Joshi 1983:7).

"It is a very close community," Tsering says. "People stick with each other. If the children become too interested in Western things, unlike the parents in Jawalakhel, here we have enough control to remind them of the importance of Tibetan culture." The seventh-grade girls in the camp wear their hair in the most recent styles of Kathmandu, and they do what they can to make their school uniforms as fashionable as possible. A Tibetan girl working in a trekking store in Kathmandu guessed that when these girls come into Kathmandu, they probably like to go shopping and eat ice cream. In fact, the girls from Tashi Palkhiel said, on their visits to Kathmandu they go to the stupas to pray. Most of them attended the ceremony at Bodh Gaya in the winter of 1985. Although they did not fully understand the teachings, simply having had the opportunity to receive the blessing of the Dalai Lama made the long journey worthwhile. Born and raised in Nepal, these girls immediately and emphatically state that they are Tibetan.

One reason Tashi Palkhiel has managed to avoid the internal conflict found in Dhorpatan and in some of the other settlements is because almost all of the residents of the camp are from the same area in Tibet, and because they continue to be led by the man who had been their leader in Tibet. "Dhorpatan will never progress because everyone is from different places," a Tibetan who assisted the Swiss in both settlements remarked. "There are Khampas, nomads, etcetera. No one listens to each other. Tashi Palkhiel, on the other hand, succeeds because most people are from the same area and listen to their leader." Furthermore, Tashi Palkhiel is close enough to Pokhara that the Tibetans have the benefits of a city: stores with a fairly wide selection of affordable goods, electric lights, running water, kerosene stoves, and a mission hospital. As tourism grows in Pokhara, opportunities for economic advancement beyond being "something sellers" become available; these opportunities in turn attract younger refugees educated in India. The settlement is isolated enough that the refugees remain a separate group; the strong bond of the Tibetan community makes them reluctant to leave.

Together the community has worked and continues to work to create the conditions by which the Tibetan ideals of cultural preservation can be in accord with the economic realities of their life. Tibetan communities across Nepal are struggling to achieve a similar balance.

Part Four

The Ideal and the Reality

> Living conditions are now much better, but from the heart, our feelings haven't changed, we are still thinking that one day we will return to Tibet. Many people have built houses and purchased land. It is not that they have forgotten about going back to Tibet and want to settle here permanently, but because they have to run their lives according to the rules of the land.
>
> —*Samten Dorje, private carpet factory owner*

Chapter 11

The Ideal

Tibetans moving to Nepal from India often remark that the refugees in Nepal, in Thamel in particular, are overly preoccupied with business and with making money. It is rumored that when the businesspeople in Nepal see newcomers from Tibet they save their welcomes and first ask, "Do you have any antiques to sell?" Refugees in Dharmsala, these same Tibetans say, discuss the administration, their jobs, and the future of Tibet; those in Nepal are said to be less interested in these issues, preferring to talk only of the carpet industry.

The Tibetans criticizing the refugees in Nepal are concerned about the long-term impact that growing up in such an environment will have on young children. They fear that the singlemindedness with which these Tibetans seek a profit will eventually begin to undermine Tibetan culture. The deputy director of education says:

> Living with parents who are always running after making money affects the children and their culture because they tend simply to work to make their own living better and better without thinking about freedom and nationality. You are no longer as happy with your situation and you always want more, more. You lose the values of Buddhism; if these values are lost among Tibetans, the disintegration of the culture will follow.

"Sometimes money weakens the spirit," Rinchen Dharlo observes, "but without money and the education and knowledge that money can buy, Tibetans can do nothing to help their cause." With money and an understanding of how the world in the twentieth century works, they can.

"Many Tibetans in India complain about those in the West," comments Tenzin Geyche, the Dalai Lama's personal secretary.

> Many in the West complain about those in India and Nepal. I feel that the two sides do not really try to understand the conditions that prevail in a particular place. Similarly, if in Kathmandu most Tibetans are in business, I do not think you can say to Tibetans in Nepal, "You are only business minded." If the West is very fast and a Tibetan lives there for five or six years and becomes very fast, you cannot say you are very unlike Tibetans, you have become very Westernized.

The refugees in Nepal have had to adapt to the rules of the land, rules that are different from those in India. They have tremendous economic freedom, yet they are forbidden to engage in any form of political organization. They can set up private shops without a permit, but they cannot own land, export goods, or travel to a foreign country unless they are Nepalese citizens. "We may be more businesslike in Nepal," says Wangchuck Tsering, who has lived in Nepal for 15 years,

> but that's because its easier to do, that's all we have to do. We have no land, no opportunities for involvement in social or political organizations. I can't send my children to schools in Dharmsala, I'm not satisfied with the Tibetan schools in Nepal, and to send my children to India, I need money.

Such freedoms and limitations are the prevailing conditions to which Tenzin Geyche refers; they must be understood before drawing any conclusions as to how well the ideals espoused by the Dalai Lama have been integrated into the lives of the refugees in Nepal.

*   *   *   *   *

> Tibetans hope the Chinese will change but more important, Tibetans believe that human determination will overcome and the flame of truth will flourish.
> —*Dalai Lama, quoted in Avedon*, In Exile from the Land of Snows

The Dalai Lama fled his nation on the night of 17 March 1959 because he realized he could be of greater use to his people outside the grasp of the Chinese. In the years following his departure, the Chinese have systematically worked to eradicate his culture and, it seems, his people. Refugees believe that recent events in Tibet, particularly the forced migration of Han Chinese to the Tibetan plateau, are far more threatening to the survival of their culture than even the rampant destruction of the Cultural Revolution. And they recognize that only the refugees can prevent the Chinese from succeeding with their efforts. "Those in Tibet trust in the Tibetans outside of Tibet very much because they know that the refugees are free whereas the Tibetans inside Tibet are bound, they cannot move," Karma said quietly. "So they can only hope and trust that His Holiness and the Tibetans in exile will be able to liberate them." "In exile we are in a free country and we can do each and every kind of practice," explains an exiled Tibetan. "The Chinese want to eliminate the name of Tibet from this world — if we don't preserve our culture in India and Nepal, then what will happen?"

If the Tibetans in Tibet accept Chinese rule, if they transfer their loyalty from the Dalai Lama and the government-in-exile where it now lies to the Communist government in Peking, the exiles' struggle for an independent Tibet is no longer necessary. "If the Tibetans inside Tibet agree that the Chinese government is okay, then we have nothing to do," Karma says. "We are not fighting against the Chinese just to have the privilege or seat for the Tibetans-in-exile or the Dalai Lama. We are doing what we are for the Tibetans inside of Tibet." The Dalai Lama explains:

> The reason we appeal to other nations is not because we want to go back and the Chinese are not allowing [us] in. . . . The real issues are the feelings and welfare of the six million Tibetans still left in Tibet. Why should an alien rule be forced upon them? Why shouldn't they have the choice of holding their own beliefs, traditions, culture, and identity?
>
> If those six million Tibetans are really happy and contented we would be prepared to return and accept whatever status the majority of them are prepared to give us. (Dalai Lama 1980:118)

The dramatic increase in political unrest in Tibet since September 1987 belies any Chinese claims that their rule has been accepted by the Tibetans. Monks, nuns, and students are crying out for independence; they are denouncing the Chinese military invasion and condemning the brutal repression of their peaceful demonstrations. Hundreds of Tibetans have been arrested or wounded in these demonstrations; increasing numbers are being killed. The Tibetan Nationalist Group of the Three Provinces appealed to the US Congress and the United Nations Human Rights Committee on 1 September 1988:

> The Chinese do not place any value on Tibetan lives. The human rights violations in Tibet are so numerous that they cannot all be told. . . . We are very grateful to those peace-loving countries and their leaders who support the Tibetans' just cause. Again, we urge you to strongly support all three provinces of Tibet in our struggle to regain independence under the leadership of His Holiness the Dalai Lama, so that we may enjoy the same rights as people in the free world. Please, please, please give us your firm support.

The Dalai Lama has said, "We are not against the Chinese. . . . We are only trying to gain our rights, to save our people, and to preserve our Buddhist dharma."

Every refugee inherits a profund sense of responsiblity to uphold these values and to live up to the trust of those in Tibet. It is up to every individual to keep Tibetan national and cultural identity alive. An understanding of this responsibility and a sense of the urgency involved must be instilled in the generation of children now in school. If it is not, if the flame of nationality is lost, than the hope of a freed Tibet will slip away: the refugees will have betrayed their countrymen and will have cut the bonds that also serve to hold together their cultural integrity.

Chapter 12

The Economic Reality

> The people are moving to the cities. Its happening all over; who is going to grow the food?
>
> — *Father Moran*

Chialsa, 1986: At five o'clock in the morning, 55-year-old Lobsang begins to stir. He climbs out from under a tattered, hand-woven wool blanket and pulls on his sheep-skin pants. He relights the butter lamp on the altar by his bed and quietly opens the door to the gonpa so as not to wake his daughter and her newborn baby. He slips through the small, dark room where his son-in-law and grandson lie sleeping, stopping briefly to adjust the blanket over the small child, and picks up two plastic water jugs from the adjoining kitchen. He unlocks the door and walks along the dirt path by the schoolyard to the latrine. After filling the jugs with water from the nearby stream, he returns to the house and blows on the still smoldering sticks in the small mud stove. He adds more wood — an expensive necessity used as sparingly as possible — and puts on the water for tea. He mixes flour and water together in a bowl, and slowly kneads the mixture on the wooden chopping board, ignoring his daughter in the next room, who is now yelling at her husband to get out of bed. As he makes the tea, he softly murmurs "Om Mani Padme Hum." Tea ready, he rolls out the dough into flat chapatis and cooks them on a metal plate.

Lobsang was a cook in Tibet. When he arrived in Chialsa 25 years ago, he went to work in the cooperative restaurant opened by the Swiss aid workers. Four years ago, when his daughter married, he left the tea shop to cook for her family so that she could keep weaving in the carpet factory.

Day after day he methodically goes about his chores. He goes outside only to check his small garden and to fetch water; he is constantly cleaning or cooking or sweeping, doing everything slowly and thoughtfully. At night, when his work is done, he sits on the bed in the kitchen in the dark, rotating his prayer beads and whispering "Om Mani Padme Hum."

He has seen the Dalai Lama once in Tibet. He has not received the Dalai Lama's blessing since, because he does not have enough money to travel to India. It would be good, Lobsang says, to see him at least once more before his own death.

Lobsang's son-in-law, Phuntsok, teaches in the school. In the morning, as he waits for his bread, Phuntsok fiddles with the radio, stopping here and there to listen to bits of news or to a Hindi song he likes. When the bread comes, he picks at it, quickly swallows his tea, and heads off to ring the bell for morning exercises at school. When classes begin, Phuntsok squats under the tree outside the classroom, waiting before going in to teach. He eventually strolls in, writes the lesson on the board, and waits for the bell to ring. During lunch break, he plays with the radio again while he waits to go back to school, where he passes the time until the bell rings and it is time to go home. At night in bed, he fiddles with the radio waiting to go to sleep, waiting for the next day, waiting to move to Kathmandu.

*   *   *   *   *

In July 1962, Thupten Nyima, a Tibetan from Shakar district in Tibet, arrived in Namche Bazaar with instructions from Dharmsala to coordinate the resettlement of the refugees scattered in the Khumbu Valley. He discussed plans with the Tibetans living in Namche to start a small sweater-knitting and blanket-weaving factory. The Sherpas, however, were already weaving blankets and belts of Tibetan wool for local distribution; the Tibetan enterprise would interfere with this business. The refugees decided it would be best to move, and so Thupten Nyima sent surveyors through Solu Khumbu to find possible sites for relocation.

Eventually the surveyors selected a site on an empty ridge in the middle hills below Mount Everest. *Ja Sa*, meaning "rainbow place," was the original name of this area. Many years ago a Sherpa monk had passed through the Solu valley looking for a place to build his monastery. While at the site of the present gonpa, he looked out and saw a rainbow arching across the valley below. He took this as an auspicious sign that if he built his monastery there, it would benefit a large number of people. The Swiss, who arrived soon after the Tibetans, had trouble pronouncing Ja Sa, the name of the monastery, and recommended it be changed to Chialsa. Since they were providing quite a bit of money, the name was altered as they requested.

From the top of the ridge, a 45-minute walk above where the Tibetans eventually settled, the tip of Mount Everest is visible on a clear day. Much of the forest on this ridge was destroyed in a fire in 1978; the rest of the wood has gradually been burned to boil water and dye wool. Deforestation is one of Nepal's most urgent problems as its steadily increasing population continues to terrace the steep mountain slopes and use the trees for fuel. It is said, only half jokingly, that the government could plant a national flag on a sand bar that has formed where the Ganges, which drains the Himalayan mountains, enters the Indian Ocean. Across the valley from Chialsa, amidst the green fields and forest, lies a huge stretch of rocks and sand where a chunk of land no longer held firm by plant roots toppled to the river below.

Tibetans in Namche loaded tents, bedrolls, and whatever valuables they had not yet sold onto their backs and walked three days south to Chialsa. The children stayed behind, attending classes and living with those Tibetans who had decided to remain on their own. Upon arriving in Chialsa, the refugees cleared the land and immediately began building one-story mud and stone houses with funds provided by the ICRC. Dr. Eklehoff, the ICRC representative, helped organize the settlement and distribute food, medicine, and clothing.

A small crafts center was opened with 25 weavers in a Sherpa house rented with funds from ICRC. By the end of 1965, more than 55 weavers were employed. Skilled Sherpa laborers were hired to build several long buildings of mud and stone to provide the handicraft center with a permanent home.

Soon after the houses were completed, the children and their two teachers came down from Namche and moved into a stone and mud schoolhouse. Men who chose not to weave carpets built benches, desks, tables, and blackboards for the school. Since the school was included under Father Moran's committee, the children studied English, Tibetan, Nepalese, mathematics, and science, as did the students in Jawalakhel. After classes students planted, weeded, and harvested a vegetable garden under the direction of Tsering Choedak, the English and math teacher, now the manager of the Dhorpatan settlement. Upon completing the fifth grade, many of the children, girls in particular, were sent to weave carpets in the handicraft center. Since Chialsa was included in the group of SATA camps, the center received supplies, salaries, and orders from the Carpet Trading Company. Raw wool was carried by Nepalese porters from the nearest road, which at that time was a 10-day walk; the finished carpets

Children in every Tibetan school are led through exercises each morning. The order of these exercises reflects the organization and overall quality of the school, both of which improved dramatically when a new principal arrived in Chialsa in 1986. ©Ann Forbes

were then carried back out.

After some initial problems getting started, the Chialsa handicraft center "grew from scratch to be one of the best-managed and best-quality producing centers in Nepal." Tashi Phuntsok, the center's accountant from 1968 to 1973, said, "These were the bright years of Chialsa: the settlement was prospering from every side and the handicraft center was really flourishing. The carpets from Chialsa always won the quality award among the CTC group. The center was at a real height." Two hostels, sponsored by Mrs. Tigerstadt, a volunteer from Norway, were added to the school so that Tibetan children whose families had remained in Namche could study in a Tibetan school. Classes in English, Tibetan, Nepali, and math were held at night for the carpet weavers. After night school, all the settlers gathered in the field by the factory where they joined in a circle and danced the traditional dances of Ting'gri into the early hours of morning. The camp had the most active drama group of any refugee settlement in Nepal. It regularly staged Tibetan operas; many members who have since moved to Kathmandu are the mainstay of the Tibetan Opera Group, which performs at all of the major Tibetan functions in Boudha and Swayambhu.

The clinic opened by the Swiss was overseen by a Tibetan trained at a mission hospital in a village two days' trip from Chialsa. In addition, a hospital with Western facilities and a Sherpa doctor trained in Kathmandu was opened one hour away, in Phaplu. To prevent the refugees from being solely dependent on their weaving salaries, the Swiss arranged for each family to have fields in which to cultivate potatoes, wheat, or barley; the Tibetans, however, have chosen to plant only potatoes. They are unable to grow other crops, they say, because they have no livestock and thus no manure for fertilization, no fences to keep out the Sherpas' livestock, and, perhaps most important, no interest.

During this period, a Tibetan from Chialsa attended a meeting of the Council of Home Affairs in Dharmsala. He said that, at the time, Chialsa was the best camp anywhere. The refugees had everything they needed: steady employment, a good school, good health facilities, free housing, and lots of cultural activities. "Perhaps," Tashi said, "it was reaching a saturation point. It had reached the top and we couldn't hope to make it better without supporting developments."

During the winter school closes for vacation and families travel to Kathmandu to see relatives and visit the stupas. Every year, one or two families did not return; those who did spoke of the electricity in Kathmandu, which enabled weavers to work longer hours and thus make more money, and the cars, running water, and stoves that made daily chores so much easier. The next year, several more families would visit the city and a few more would not return.

In the 27 years he has lived in Chialsa, Lobsang has been to Kathmandu twice. Aside from visiting the stupas, he does not like the city at all. It is too crowded and noisy; the air is dirty and the food is bad. He, like most older Tibetans, prefers Chialsa, which has good air, food, and water, and where it is peaceful and the weather is cool.

Lobsang's daughter and her husband, on the other hand, speak longingly of moving to Kathmandu. In Chialsa, their combined salary is barely sufficient to feed their family. The nearest medical facility in Kathmandu is a 15-minute cab ride away. The standard of the Chialsa school has deteriorated under the Nepalese administration. They also want to go for the same reason that villagers throughout Asia are moving to the cities: the attractions of their culture and traditional way of life are fading against the bright lights and vast opportunities promised by the city.

If economics and the allure of the West were not enough to convince refugees to leave Chialsa, during the late 1970s widespread rumors circulated of the disappearance of large sums of money from the carpet factory accounts. Funds sent from CTC earmarked to be distributed among handicraft center workers as their annual bonus were instead put toward trying to offset the deficit, and the workers were forced to give up the additional income. Lobsang and other older Tibetans shrug their shoulders at the whispers of corruption and the complaints about mismanagement. His son-in-law and other government-in-exile staff in the settlement, however, speak bitterly of these events and blame the most recent manager for Chialsa's decline.

The rumors of corruption sped up the slow but steady migration to Kathmandu; its occurrence underscores the limitations of ideas and plans introduced into a community by outsiders. For the most part, the Tibetans in Chialsa came from the same region — Ting'gri, in southeastern Tibet — but had lived as separate and independent households there. Each family was an economic unit, and few shared financial or managerial responsibilities with others. On arriving in exile, however, they were suddenly forced to become a community; their lives were no longer independent, and the fate of each was entangled in that of the other. Feelings of tolerance and respect had to be replaced by those of trust. Relationships that had been based on independence had to evolve into those of cooperation. This transition did not occur as smoothly or as completely as the Swiss may have hoped in any of the camps. Chialsa's isolation seems to have made the impact more severe than in the other, more urban settlements.

In 1979 the population of Chialsa was 600. A 1986 census showed the population to be 261, 100 being more than 45 years old; only 40 were between the ages of 25 and 40. The settlement is now dotted with empty stone houses; the windows and doors are boarded up, the stone walls are falling down, and the prayer flags, which haven't been replaced for years, are tattered and worn, rags flapping silently in the wind. In the spring of 1986 a new manager finally agreed to go to Chialsa. He left after three months with no explanation, and went to Dharmsala, where he pleaded for a transfer. The manager was told that if he agreed to return for the remainder of the year, he would be relocated. It was clear to the refugees, however, that he was only biding his time. Sonam Tsering, a monk from the Institute of Buddhist Studies in Varanasi, agreed to be principal of the school. His untiring zeal reinstilled energy into the cold, dank classrooms. Yet the school's success ultimately depends on the economic status of the camp; if only older refuees remain in Chialsa, Sonam's ideas will have no place there.

At this same time, in an attempt to halt the migration to Kathmandu, new houses were built, electricity from a nearby hydroelectric plant was installed, and alternative economic opportunities, such as growing apple trees, were introduced. Those remaining in Chialsa, however, say these improvements came too late: most of the capable, ambitious refugees were already long gone. Tibetans today say that three years ago the settlement felt like home; they enjoyed living there and were optimistic about the future. Now the camp has a sense of impermanence and its future is insecure. Lobsang's daughter stays in Chialsa only because that is her father's wish. Her husband, who was sent to this village by the Tibetan government-in-exile, is impatient to move. Together, their evenings are often spent in terse whispers and uncomfortable gaps of silence as they weigh each side of their dilemma in the darkness of the tiny mud and stone room. (The following year they moved to Kathmandu. Three months later, Lobsang died.)

A 50-year-old woman who has not left Chialsa since her arrival in 1962 periodically receives messages from her sister living in Kathmandu to come join her in the city, where life is so much easier. The woman remains in Chialsa, however. "If you live separately, as do so many people in Kathmandu, and go about your own business," she says, "you lose contact with Tibetans. It is better to stay in camps with other refugees, this is what Yeshi Norbu [the Dalai Lama] has said. If not, what are Tibetans?" "We're not like Westerners or Nepalese," another Tibetan says. "We have a very big problem — we don't have our country so it is important to stay together. When Tibetans stay individually, there is a loss of community; we can't do that yet; it's not the right time."

As manager of CTC, Tashi Phuntsok is financially responsible for Chialsa's future. Because of the expense of transporting the raw materials and the finished product to and from Kathmandu by porters, the factory is operating under a tremendous financial loss. CTC could invest this money far more effectively elsewhere, but making a profit is not the sole function of the government-in-exile factories. The first priority of all factories under the Council of Home Affairs is to provide employment for and to look after the welfare of the Tibetans settled in the camps. As long as a community of Tibetans remains in Chialsa, it is the responsibility of CTC to support it.

Tibetan leaders strongly believe that they should continue to assist those who need their help, but they do not try to prevent those who are capable of settling on their own from doing so. If the land belonged to the refugees, then, Rinchen Dharlo says he would be concerned that so many are leaving. As refugees, however, their identity as Tibetans is not wrapped up in the land or the place in which they have resettled; instead, it has necessarily become something that is less tangible, something that they can carry with them to Nepal, to India, to the United States. As long as their sense of being Tibetan and their commitment to the Tibetan cause is not compromised in the move to Kathmandu, then the decline of Chialsa, or of any other settlement, is not seen as a threat to the ideals that the refugees are to uphold.

* * * * *

There is a danger of forgetting our main course, our main cause. When you are very poor you are always thinking "I am a Tibetan, I'm very poor. Tibet must get its independence, otherwise I am not able to live." Then there is a stage when you know you are a Tibetan but you are doing business and 24 hours a day you are thinking about how to make more money, I think you somewhat forget about being Tibetan and being poor. Then after a while you pass that stage and when you do business you earn money but you are more relaxed and you know what you are doing. I think then there is again a stage when this idea "I am Tibetan and I am a refugee" is always there. So I do not regard this — economic success — as a problem. (Karma, secretary of Snow Lion Foundation)

Some of the refugees leaving Chialsa and other remote settlements join one of the Tibetan settlement handicraft centers. More often, however, they weave in private factories for several years before opening their own carpet shop or small weaving factory. Since housing in the government-in-exile settlements is only available to those who work in the handicraft centers, these Tibetans rent rooms from Nepalese in Boudha or in Jawalakhel, where a number of Tibetans have settled. A growing number of these refugees are also moving to Thamel, the tourist mecca of Kathmandu, in order to open restaurants, guest houses, trekking stores, and carpet shops.

Tsering Dolkar is 20 years old. She wears her long black hair loose or pulled back in a pony tail. She wears tight jeans and a T-shirt or button-down shirt with a lightweight Patagonia jacket when the weather is cool. She seems to use more English slang than many native speakers, and phrases such as "you know" and "like" punctuate her speech. She emphasizes her words in a typically American way and gestures with her hands to drive home her point.

She runs her family's trekking equipment shop, located in the heart of Thamel. Many of the other trekking stores are managed by older Sherpa or Tibetan men, and travelers often think that they will get a better deal because Tsering is a young girl. They have no such luck. She runs a very good shop; her store is constantly busy because she sells and rents equipment and buys secondhand belongings. "She is a very astute businesswoman," a Peace Corps volunteer says. "She knows what price she wants and she won't bargain; she knows the names of all American manufacturers and their prices." She likes working in a trekking store because she meets lots of people, "especially famous climbers." She speaks French, German, Nepali, Hindi, English, and is thinking of studying Japanese. "We get a lot of Japanese customers. They think I'm Japanese so they speak to me in their language and I hate not being able to answer them. I feel so stupid, you know." When she's not working, which is not very often, she likes to read novels, talk with her friends, and go running.

Tsering comes from an influential Tibetan family that was wealthy even when in Tibet. Her parents fled in 1959 and went to Delhi, where her father worked for the government-in-exile. They moved to Nepal in 1970 to join an aunt who had married a Nepalese. When she moved to Kathmandu, Tsering had to relearn the Tibetan language because she had previously attended an Indian school and could speak only Hindi. Her parents enrolled her as a boarding student at St. Mary's "because it was the best school in Nepal." St. Mary's, the sister school of St. Xavier's, which was started by Father Moran, is run by Catholic nuns. The queen of Nepal graduated from this school and the princess is now a student. Although Tsering's parents lived less than five miles away, she was sent as a boarding student because "my parents were afraid I would get run over getting on and off the buses. Everyone was so busy in those days, no one was organized. It was better for me; I could have a set time to study, you know." Tsering remembers seeing a few other Tibetan girls in the school but her friends were mostly Nepalese. In the eighth grade, when she was old enough to travel to school on her own, she became a day student so that she could live with her family.

Tsering is the child of that class of refugees who, because they have established successful private businesses in Kathmandu, can afford to send their children to private schools. The parents of these children were born in Tibet and are still very traditional. The women wear chubbas, finger prayer beads as they sit in their shops, socialize primarily with Tibetans, and, although many can speak English, prefer to converse in Tibetan.

It is a different case with their children, who have been born and raised into the upper economic class of Nepal. Tsering, who appears quite Western, remarked that the amount she knows about her culture is unusual for this class. "If you see the other side you'll get a shock," she said, talking about those Tibetans her age who have gone to boarding school in India. "They don't know much, I doubt they can even read or write Tibetan. [Written Tibetan is far more complicated than colloquial Tibetan.] All they know is that they are Buddhists. They're so into fashion it makes me sick."

On vacations these Tibetans return home to their families in Thamel, where they play tennis and basketball; they eat in restaurants and stay out late watching videos. They discuss business opportunities with their parents and their peers, and they speak a mixture of Tibetan and English.

"When children come home from an English school," Ugen Tsering, the owner of Utse's, whose sons attend school in Darjeeling, says, "They don't work, they just eat with a knife and fork and don't wash their clothes. They go to study, to play, and to meet their friends."

A number of these younger Tibetans attended a Tibetan wedding in Patan, near Jawalakhel, in 1986. The wedding began early in the day. Some guests arrived in time for a mid-morning cup of tea and then sat down to begin gambling. Throughout the morning more guests filtered in; many joined the gamblers, while others — women and children and those men who did not gamble — sat gossiping in groups on the floor. At 11:30, the bride and groom, dressed in elaborately decorated silk chubbas and wearing traditional Tibetan hats, walked onto a stage at the far end of the hall. They sat side by side behind two knee-high tables with their heads down. Their parents and relatives walked onto the stage to offer the couple white scarves and then took their seats on either side. A man wearing a red silk chubba and two women carrying teapots filled with chang stepped out in front of the couple. The man chanted and sang for their happiness and good luck, and the women passed bowls of chang, which the family members drank down to the bottom. Prayers completed, the guests formed a long line to greet the couple and offer scarves and presents to the family.

Immediately following the brief ceremony, a buffet lunch of rice, meat, and vegetable dishes was served. After lunch, the guests and wedding party returned to their cards, their friends, their children, or their jobs. In the evening another buffet was served and bowls of chang were passed by friends of the family; they sang drinking songs to embarrass reluctant drinkers into finishing their cups. Shortly thereafter, a group of older Tibetans, their long braids coiled around their heads, joined arms in a circle and began to dance. Several older women entered the circle, crying out the melancholy chants to the muffled beat of the drum. More and more people joined in; the older men, many of whom had moved down from Chialsa, were the obvious leaders: they chose the dances and set the pace. Others — the younger men and women, in particular — were more hesitant, and intently and shyly followed the steps of their neighbors. Most of the carpet sellers and the students from Indian schools did not dance, but instead continued gambling or sat in groups sipping beer, chang, or whiskey.

After two hours or so of the traditional dances, the crowd began to dwindle until only the original group of older men remained. Someone slipped a Michael Jackson tape into the tape deck and a handful of boys with short, styled hair began to dance. A few girls in Western clothing joined in, and soon a small crowd was dancing away to the sounds of the West. The older Tibetans went outside, and only schoolchildren and young men and women stayed around to watch the dancers. "The young generation is really forgetting," an older Tibetan woman remarked. "They like pop music, not Tibetan music.... Some children do not agree that dances and performing the morning prayers are important ... but if they don't know, they will not be able to teach their children."

Tsering Dolkar attributes her own knowledge and appreciation for Tibetan culture to having lived at home after the eighth grade. Although during the daytime she spoke English and Nepali and socialized with Nepalese students, at night her parents discussed Tibetan issues. Tibetan friends and relatives from India stopped by on their way to visit Tibet. As they did their chores, her mother would explain what had happened in Tibet, what their relatives in Tibet were doing, and what must be done to regain Tibetan independence. Together they listened to tapes of speeches by the Dalai Lama. She accompanied her parents on holidays when they visited the monasteries and stupas, and she assisted her mother when they invited monks to pray in their home. Her younger brothers have been sent to India so they can obtain a good education. Tsering comments, "In our home you're seeing it, too. I don't know that much about Tibetan culture to be honest. But compared to my brothers, I know a little more, and compared to my older brother, my younger brother doesn't know *anything.*"

In Tsering's opinion, the increasing emphasis on education at the expense of an understanding of Tibetan culture is cause for concern. "Its not okay!" she exclaims. "Like at Bodh Gaya when the Dalai Lama gave the Kalachakra Initiation, my mother was telling me, on the one hand there are real devotees, real holy people from Tibet — old people and people my mom and dad's age — and on the other there was my age group and they weren't there for the prayer, you know, and that's kind of hurting." Tsering, as do many other Tibetans, feels that something must be done to withstand the dissipation of her culture; she believes it is up to the parents to assume the burden of the responsibility:

> The parents should tell them to do the holy things in the morning — the children would do it, if not by liking at least by force. They would do it and do it until it becomes a habit and then they'll start to wonder, Why am I doing this? When I was little, I'd obey my mother and do all the prayer things, but now I've become really lazy and I just don't do them. Like five months ago I started saying, you know, "Why am I not doing this anymore? Because I'm changing, everything's changing and speeding so fast and I say I should go back to my whatever."

Education is not the only arena in which this class of refugees is being forced to choose between being Tibetan and being successful. Legal status, too, is becoming a matter of concern for Tibetans in Nepal. Do these refugees remain "stateless people," residing temporarily in a foreign country while holding on to the hope of eventually returning to their country? Or do they become citizens of Nepal and thus acquire the right to own land, export goods, and travel to foreign countries? As with education, this is not simply a black-and-white question. The Dalai Lama espouses the ideal:

> We are political refugees so we have to concern ourselves with the Tibetans who are inside Tibet. As a free spokesman for Tibetan people my main post is for the Tibetan people there. Of course. Now everybody knows that the Tibetans inside Tibet are absolutely loyal to Tibet and are trusting those Tibetans who are outside Tibet. I think when the situation concerning citizenship comes up, individual cases are all right. But [if] the community as a whole were to become citizens then that may create the wrong impression inside Tibet. [They may think] that those Tibetans who are outside Tibet have given up their responsibility, their hope. That is the point. We have to avoid giving such an impression to the Tibetans who are still inside Tibet.

"If refugees have become citizens of another country, then naturally the Tibetans in Tibet would lose their faith," Rinchen Dharlo says. "We left Tibet not to become Nepalese citizens; we came to fight for our country." The owner of a carpet exporting factory's responsibilities necessarily include marketing those carpets. The markets are in Europe, and travel to Europe requires a passport. Thus, in meeting the inescapable demands of their reality, leading citizens who in turn set an example for the other refugees are becoming citizens of the country in which they are exiled.

Despite the increasing number of entrepreneurs in the Kathmandu valley, the most respected and effective means of living up to the responsibility the refugees inherit as Tibetans is to work for the government-in-exile in a government carpet factory, a school, or a government office. Unfortunately the personal sacrifices required by a life of service to the community do not make the altruistic route an easy or a practical choice for the average Tibetan. Those who work for the government cannot afford the luxuries that come from private business. One leading Tibetan who was educated and trained by the Swiss to take over one of the settlement carpet factories continues to work for the government:

> I feel like I have an obligation to work for the Tibetan community because what I am is thanks to the Tibetan government. They gave me formal and practical training. I don't work for the pay, but I feel that now is time that people who have the knowhow should come forward and work. Perhaps in the future they may not need me but now the government cannot afford highly qualified teachers.

He works half a day; in the other half, he manages his private factory. His private work provides him with the money to feed and educate his family and thus allows him to continue his "social work." It supplies him with the material goods which then enable him to uphold his responsibility to the

Tibetan community. This Tibetan is able to balance his private and public lives. A few Tibetans have followed his example; the majority, however, are making a choice.

Lobsang Nyima worked for the government-in-exile in India for 15 years. In 1981 he was transferred to the settlement in Jawalakhel. The previous managers of this settlement were rumored to have been more interested in furthering their personal fortunes through private business than in improving the living standard in the settlement. "I am not like the past managers of Jawalakhel," Lobsang assured a crowd of carpet weavers, spinners, and office staff. "I will dedicate all of my time to turning Jawalakhel into the model refugee camp in Nepal. I don't need to do private business; I can support my family on the government salary alone."

On another occasion, Lobsang said his two most important goals were to make the Tibetan community in which he works a perfect one and to provide his two boys with a good education and his family with a good life. On the government salary of US$75–85 per month—$50 of which is used to pay the rent on their three-room apartment—it is difficult, if not impossible, to realize these two goals simultaneously.

A year and a half after Lobsang's arrival, he opened a carpet shop. Every morning before work he visits private Tibetan factories to purchase rugs for his wife to sell in their store; he spends his days managing the carpet factory. At the end of the day he rushes home to cook dinner, carry carpets to his shop, and look after his two sons.

In the 1960s the Swiss selected a number of Tibetan children to go overseas for education and training. Although a few of these children went permanently, the majority were expected to return and apply their knowledge to improving conditions in the Tibetan communities. One such Tibetan who chose to return from Denmark to work for the government now regrets his decision. "I simply made a mistake, I made the wrong choice," he says. "At that time I felt a strong drive to work for my people. I didn't know how hard life in India and Nepal was." Tenzin Geyche, the Dalai Lama's translator, explains the situation quite clearly:

> My friends feel that young people aren't working for the government because of a lack of determination and nationalism, but I feel that there is another factor. Of course it is important to have some sort of patriotism or loyalty or nationalism when you want to work for a Tibetan establishment. But often whether you are willing to continue is governed by whether the facilities are good, whether the salary is sufficient. Frankly speaking, many young Tibetans are getting used to a fairly comfortable life. If someone is in the teaching field and if he finds it difficult to live on 600 rupees, even if he is slightly interested, he may leave because he is not able to live the kind of life he wants to live on that kind of salary.

Among Tibetans, the sense of belonging, the sense of pride that you are a Tibetan is quite strong. No one can live on determination and loyalty for 30 to 40 years. In the beginning maybe 90 percent was patriotism, the morale was high and so they didn't care about living conditions. After 10 or 15 years, they had to strike a balance.

*   *   *   *   *

The financial success of the class of refugees in Thamel does not represent the situation for the average Tibetan in Nepal, nor even that of most Tibetans in the Kathmandu valley. The level of their success, however, does affect the economic standard to which many Tibetans in Nepal aspire. Every community develops important role models who influence the choices made by the individual members. The circumstances of the Tibetan refugees living in Nepal have created different and opposing forms of symbolism: on one hand is the cultural integrity as reflected by the life and words of the Dalai Lama, and on the other are the more Western ideals unavoidably brought on by increased prosperity. Each year more Tibetans leave their villages to seek out the brother, uncle, or friend who is more prosperous in Kathmandu. What will happen, one wonders, when there are no more Tibetans in the border areas to lead the younger, more modern generation through the dances, to perform in the opera - to provide an alternative to the path pursued by the carpet entrepreneurs?

The Tibetans of Nepal are exposed more and more to values other than those presented by the Dalai Lama, and they are challenged, more so than any other Tibetan group, to enter the twenty-first century with their culture and identity left intact. Their path is a tell-tale road for the future of Tibetan culture.

Chapter 13

The Political Reality

> When the people around the children are not concerned with their nation and with patriotism, then they just forget about it and go their own way. In India, where people are free to do any political activities, Tibetans are always concerned with Tibet's future, with when Tibet will be free, and with what is going on with Tibetans around the world. So the children in India naturally have the feeling that one day they must save their country and be a pure Tibetan.... If we were given the opportunity to do political work and demonstrate in Nepal, naturally Tibetans in Nepal would give more attention to Tibetan freedom and nationality.
> — *Wangdu Chodak, teacher, Atisha Primary School*

On 20 January 1981, while on a pilgrimage to Bodh Gaya, the Dalai Lama crossed the border of Nepal to pay a brief visit to the shrine built at Lumbini, the site of the Buddha's birth. This was the Dalai Lama's first and only visit to Nepal in 27 years. The visit lasted eight hours and no forms were filled out to record its ever having taken place (Avedon 1984:183).

For days Tibetan refugees from throughout Nepal traveled to Lumbini to welcome the bodhisattva and to receive his blessing. All of the buses in Kathmandu were hired and any available tents rented for the occasion. The refugees lined the streets along the road entering Nepal to greet the Dalai Lama, and on foot they slowly followed his car back to the holy grounds. Seated on a brocade-covered throne made especially for the occasion, the Dalai Lama spoke to the crowds of Tibetan pilgrims gathered at the base of the stupa. He urged the refugees not to give up hope and he called upon them to keep the Tibetan cause alive. He praised them for their work in exile and emphasized the importance of leading a good and moral life. For the next several hours the Dalai Lama gave blessings to the long lines of refugees who clutched white *kha tag* to offer their leader. The Dalai Lama then ate a simple lunch prepared by Ugen Tsering, the owner of Utse's restaurant in Thamel, toured the holy grounds, and was driven out of the country.

The Chinese government refuses to acknowledge the existence of a Tibetan government-in-exile or to recognize the successful resettlement of Tibetan refugees in other countries. Although India's leaders allow the refugees to settle and have a government in their country, they do not officially recognize the government-in-exile or its claims for independence. The 1962 border war between India and China has not yet been settled; because the two countries are still officially at war, the Indians are not overly concerned with displeasing the Chinese. Nepal, on the other hand, is afraid of China's size and its expansionist motives. The king wants to maintain peaceful relations with his northern neighbor and, just as important, to continue receiving aid from the Chinese government. He already feels that the overt acceptance of this group defined by China as its enemy endangers the sensitive relationship between the two countries. Welcoming the leader of those revolutionaries into his country would be seen as an unnecessary and dangerous gesture by the king. The Dalai Lama's visit to Lumbini in 1981 was an unprecedented act of good will by King Birenda; the Tibetan leader has not returned to the kingdom since.

Another reason the Dalai Lama does not visit Nepal is that the Nepalese government cannot, or will not, take responsibility for his security. The Dalai Lama is a major obstacle to the success of China's Tibet policy, and the government-in-exile makes sure that security around its leader is tight at all times. The security department, a branch of the government in Dharmsala, carefully screens all the Dalai Lama's bodyguards, searches all visitors, and ensures that his residence is surrounded by armed guards at all times.

Although few economic or social limitations are imposed on the Tibetan refugees in Nepal, they have no political freedom. They cannot organize politically, hang propaganda signs, or demonstrate on the streets. The Nepal government has imposed these limitations because it believes that internal discord and agitation will undermine the control of the king and "might jeopardize the country's sovereignty by providing an occasion for intervention by the Chinese Communists (Harris 1973:310).

* * * * *

The existence of a Tibetan guerrilla base in the rugged mountains of Mustang in northwestern Nepal in the early 1960s only served to aggravate the Nepal government. The majority of Tibetans who formed the guerrilla group were Khampas who had fought in the resistance movement in Tibet; some had escorted the Dalai Lama from the Summer Palace to the Indian border. "We had nothing when we left," one member of the bodyguard recalls. "Even I don't have a spoon when I left Tibet. I had a gun, a blade, that's all! Where [did] we have to go? We don't know! Only that we have to fight with the Chinese, that's all we know. No one knew about going to India or Nepal, we only knew that we had to die. That's all." The Khampas saw the Dalai Lama safely into the hands of Gurkha soldiers, weeping as he crossed the border into exile; they then headed back toward Lhasa to fight the Chinese. Before leaving, the Dalai Lama gave them all a blessing and handed out charms said to protect believers from enemy bullets. "Don't fight too hard," he told them. "I need people alive."

Upon discovering that the uprising in Lhasa had already been crushed by the Chinese army and that the fighting was for the most part over, the Khampas fled in small groups, working their way back to the border and into India. Leaders of the National Volunteer Defense Army, the resistance movement led by the Dalai Lama's elder brother, Gyalo Dhundup, recruited these Khampas from road gangs scattered along the Tibetan-Indian border, where they were working in the blistering heat. Those who were strong enough immediately set out for Mustang, where they formed the core of the exile branch of the Tibetan Resistance Army.

In the early 1960s, Mustang was virtually an independent region. The district had its own king and, because of the distance to Kathmandu and the lack of passable roads, the king of Nepal could exert little influence or control over events occurring along the border. Mustang was deserted and isolated for a reason, however. Located at 12,000 feet, the landscape is barren and rocky, and the climate harsh and unforgiving. The Tibetans quickly ran out of food; they would drink huge pots of coffee to have the energy for skirmishes or scouting parties, and they chewed scraps of leather for food. They performed makeshift drills using large sticks as guns, and they slept out in the open under wool blankets. After a year or so, a group of Khampas trained by the CIA in Colorado arrived in Mustang, bringing modern military equipment, a knowledge of military strategy, and discipline. They whipped the band of guerrillas into shape and began to lead attacks on Chinese stationed along the border (Avedon 1984:123).

For eight years the Nepal government ignored the Khampa camp. Foreigners distributing international aid in Pokhara remember seeing the high-cheekboned Khampas leading trains of 20 to 30 mules into Pokhara to pick up supplies. Their rugged stature stood out distinctly among the smaller Tibetans and Nepalese living in the surrounding hills. "They were tall and they walked with their heads held high," one Westerner recalls. "They were proud; they did not want to weave carpets." Health workers did not ask for explanations when Tibetans with battle wounds showed up at clinics, and no one bothered to trace the origin of the money used to buy supplies.

By the early 1970s, however, the Nepal government had a change of heart. "No longer fearful, as it had been in the early 1960's of a Chinese attack, Nepal now wished to counter New Delhi's influence in the region by furthering ties with Peking (Avedon 1984:125). Articles appeared in *Rising Nepal,* the country's only English-language newspaper, describing the destruction inflicted by the band of Khampa guerrillas. Tibetans, who had slowly begun to feel more or less accepted in Nepalese communities, once again found themselves ostracized and discriminated against. Finally, in 1974, the Chinese government told Nepal to remove the Khampa guerrillas on its own or not to interfere when the Chinese army arrived to take care of the resistance army themselves.

The events that followed are well documented in John Avedon's *In Exile from the Land of Snows.* In the early 1970s, the CIA, which had been providing the Khampas with weapons and training, discontinued its assistance because the United States had begun talks to reopen diplomatic relations with China. A split developed within the Khampa camp itself, and Baba Yeshi, the leader of the guerrillas, surrendered to the Nepal government. With the detailed knowledge of the Khampas' military plans and their location provided by Baba Yeshi and his fellow defectors, in March 1974 the Nepal military marched into Mustang to force the Khampas to surrender. After 14 years of living on thin rice gruel and leather and sleeping on the ground through the harsh Mustang winters, the guerrillas were not simply going to hand over their weapons. They were there to attack the Chinese army and to win back their country; they would continue fighting until they died.

They ignored the speeches of the Dalai Lama's emissary, who implored that they surrender without further bloodshed. As a last resort, a government-in-exile official brought a taped message from the Dalai Lama to Mustang. The group of hardened Khampa soldiers, dressed in rags and clutching their US Army rifles, gathered on a barren knoll under a raised Tibetan flag to hear the words of their leader. They stood in silence while the voice of the Dalai Lama, a man who was first and foremost a scholar of Tibetan Buddhism and who had never fired a gun, played on. He said the Nepal was Tibet's neighbor and that the two countries had been friends since ancient times. He explained that it was no longer good to fight the

Chinese and that the guerrillas should surrender. The Dalai Lama said he needed Tibetans alive, that they could now serve their country best by helping to rebuild the Tibetan nation, and that they would be supporting, not betraying, the Tibetan cause by turning over their weapons. "When the time comes for us to fight," the Dalai Lama concluded, "we can easily get weapons from another country."

"The Dalai Lama is all-knowing," a tall and muscular ex-guerrilla explained. "When others speak we can ask for explanations and argue. With the Dalai Lama, we cannot ask why. When we were told to surrender, we shed tears of sadness but there was nothing to do, even if we have to die; it was the Dalai Lama's wish." The 978 guerrillas were disarmed and their leaders captured. Weeping, they were marched south to Pokhara — one Nepalese soldier for every five Khampas — and put into a prison on the outskirts of Pokhara for six months.

The disbanding of the guerrilla camp was "shocking"; it was a "great and sad thing," Tibetans say. Although many Tibetans knew little about the actual activities of the camp, the knowledge that the guerrilla camp existed had given Tibetans both inside and outside Tibet the reassurance that at least something concrete was being done toward regaining Tibetan independence. With the dismantling of the army, that hope was lost. Actions of unrest were replaced by speeches of restraint, and Tibetans shifted their hope from regaining their country by force to obtaining independence through more diplomatic channels.

Except for the leaders, all the Khampas were released after seven months in prison. Most of the guerrillas left immediately for India to join relatives or simply to get out of Nepal. To ensure that guerrilla activities did not simply resume elsewhere, the Nepal government assumed responsibility for the resettlement of those guerrillas who remained. The Khampas were divided into two groups: one group was sent to a small plot of land in the middle of Pokhara and the other to Jampaling, located on a hot, arid plateau above the Trisuli River, 23 km east of Pokhara.

"In the beginning," said a strong-boned Tibetan holding an umbrella to block out the unrelenting Jampaling sun, "we had a very hard time; we faced a lot of suffering. We had no food to eat and no clothes to wear." They had no houses, no work, and no money. Unaccustomed to the heat, they were highly susceptible to disease. They did not know the language nor did they understand the rules and regulations of the country; they suspected the Nepalese government and the government mistrusted them. "But who could we tell these problems to?" the Khampa asked. "We were fighting for the freedom of Tibet. No one told us to go; we chose to fight for ourselves. Who could we complain to?"

For the first two years, Lo Dik, the Tibetan organization that had supplied most of the finances for the guerrilla base from profits earned in a small restaurant in Bhutwal, a Tibetan hotel in Pokhara, and private donations, provided the relocated Khampas with food and money. Most of the younger guerrillas with money or relatives left Jampaling for Kathmandu and India. Bachelors married Tibetan women from other Pokhara camps and began to have children. The following year, the refugees built individual mud-thatched huts for their families; they also constructed a compound of single apartments for older Khampas who had no other means of support. In 1977 HCE opened a weaving center, and in 1979 a new school was constructed for the 27 students who had not been sent to school in India. In 1986 the refugees built a monastery and a new handicraft center office building. The refugees proudly claim that theirs is the best Tibetan school in Nepal, an assertion that Karma says is nearly correct. The manager of the settlement is drawing up plans for an irrigation project.

These men waged war on the army of the most populous country in the world; they survived 14 bitter winters with no shelter and few supplies, isolated in the depths of the Himalaya Mountains. Now they sit on carpets in 90-100 degree heat, spinning wool into balls. They struggle to make ends meet, and they worry over how they will feed their families if they fall sick. More than anything, they hold onto the hope of returning to a liberated Tibet.

* * * * *

"There are other things they can do to keep up the spirit besides political activities," Tenzin Geyche says. "They can hold meetings and talk about the situation in Tibet. Religious festivals are also another excellent way of keeping unity, as a way to renew this feeling of togetherness, this feeling of being Tibetan. I don't feel the political restrictions in Nepal will be harmful in the long run."

The Tibetan Youth Congress was formed in 1970 in Dharmsala by a group of young Tibetans frustrated with what they considered to be the ineffectiveness of the Tibetan government-in-exile in working toward independence. Advocating a more radical position, the group organized marches and demonstrations at the Chinese Embassy in New Delhi, called for a burning of all Chinese goods, and held a fast to increase international awareness of the atrocities committed in Tibet by the Chinese. They published their views in *Rangzen* ("Independence"), a bimonthly magazine printed in Dharmsala.

A chapter of the Youth Congress was founded in the early 1970s in Nepal. Because of Nepal's political sensitivity, members' activities were limited primarily to social service work: digging latrines, cleaning toilets, and assisting needy refugees. Every Saturday they took turns translating at the Shanta Bhawan Hospital for Tibetans who did not understand Nepali. Occasionally they put up signs, in Tibetan, denouncing the Chinese and calling for their departure from Tibet. In 1975, shortly after the disarming of the Khampa guerrillas, the most active members of the organization were arrested and put in jail. After 12 days Nepalese officials informed them that if they were ever again linked with the Youth Congress or with any other political activities in Nepal, they would immediately be sent back across the northern border to Tibet—for good. The Youth Congress still exists in Nepal, but its activities are now confined to soccer games, plays, and writing contests.

*   *   *   *   *

Tibetans rose up in arms against the Chinese on 10 March 1959. Every year since that short-lived revolution, Tibetans around the world have commemorated that day with political speeches, demonstrations at Chinese embassies, and prayers for the future independence of Tibet.

The tenth of March 1986 dawned gray and cold in Chialsa. Delicate, pale-green moss, heavy with dew, lay draped across deep pink rhododendron blossoms. The mist rolled silently around the tall pines and up the valley. The windows rattled from the steady wind. Tibetans gathered in the small, open field near the carpet factory. Women arrived in secondhand synthetic parkas from India over their traditional chubbas; older men came dressed in the traditional clothing of Ting'gri. Schoolchildren carried signs made by the factory's production manager, Tashi Dorjee, who had been active in the Tibetan Youth Congress in India before being transferred to Chialsa. The signs read, in English and Tibetan, "Tibet Belongs to Tibetans!" "According to International Law, Every Nation Has the Right to Self-Determination!" "Chinese Out of Tibet!" Four carpet weavers quickly rehearsed scales on wooden flutes and heavy drums as the children fell into line.

Led by a flag bearer carrying the Tibetan national flag and marching to the sound of the small band, the group filed up the hill and stopped at a whitewashed stone stupa on the ridge overlooking the settlement buildings. New green-and-yellow prayer flags flapped ceaselessly in the blowing white mist. Inside, a bespectacled monk pounded a large drum, clanged cymbals, and chanted vigorously, praying for the eventual independence of Tibet.

Phuntsok, a teacher at the Mount Everest School, prays with the refugee community in Chialsa on Tibetan Uprising Day. The placard, written in Tibetan, calls for China to stop human rights violations in Tibet.
©Ann Forbes

Another Tibetan flag, the display of which is forbidden in Nepal and which is unfurled in Chialsa only because of its isolation, was raised to half mast. Chanting "Om Mani Padme Hum," villagers added their prayer flags to those already raised and burned juniper branches on a white dome for incense. After the Rinpoche had led everyone in prayer, the manager read the text of the speech that the Dalai Lama was giving this same day in Dharmsala:

Our struggle is a fight for the rights that are justly upheld in today's modern times—the rights that we have inherited from our past history—and is not an act of hatred against the Chinese. . . .

The Tibetan people bravely withstood the unparalleled atrocities committed upon them. They have remained steadfast and strong. . . . And today when we commemorate the twenty-eighth anniversary of our national uprising we once again remember the brave Tibetan people. . . .

It is a mistake to presume that mere economic concessions and liberalizations can satisfy our people. The issue of Tibet is fundamentally political with international ramifications and as such only a political solution can provide a meaningful answer. (Dalai Lama 1987)

Under the shadow of the Tibetan flag flapping against a backdrop of Himalayan peaks, this small group of refugees sang out against the Chinese destruction of Tibet. They called for all Tibetans to join together under the banner of the "wish-fulfilling gem"—the Dalai Lama—and to stand united. Stepping forward and raising their arms to the sky, they cried for the Chinese to stop the destruction in Tibet. The truth will prevail, they sang, do not despair.

After the songs, the refugees pulled out fistfuls of tsampa from small leather pouches. "Lha Soooooooo." They raised the tsampa to the gods. "Lha Soooooooo." The tiny engine of the plane on its biweekly journey to distribute trekkers to Lukla groaned overhead. "Lha Soooooooo." "Lha So Gyal!!" "Victory to the gods!" Tsampa was thrown into the sky and then dumped on the nearest neighbor. The flutes and drums began and the group wound its way back down to the carpet factory offices.

Four men wearing elaborate masks and the saffron silk robes of Tibetan nobility emerged from the stockroom. On their shoulders they carried a platform with a photograph of the Dalai Lama draped with yellow silk curtains. Meanwhile, Tashi Dorjee and the settlement accountant coached the crowd of refugees in cheers: "Tibet Freedom! Who will make it? We will make it!" "China Leave Tibet!" The procession participants, led by the portrait of the Dalai Lama, marched back up the hill, shouting, "Who will win? We will win!" and stopped at the entrance to the small settlement monastery.

The office staff, schoolteachers, and monks filed into the dark monastery; the remaining villagers found a seat in the stone entryway. Seven monks, ranging from a gray-haired 60-year-old to a chubby five-year-old with his head freshly shaven, were seated on two long, maroon-cushioned benches stretching down the center of the monastery. The staff sat cross-legged on cushions set against the wall. Led by the head lama of the gonpa, everyone began chanting prayers as volunteers poured butter tea into china cups placed in front of each worshiper. The monks and staff all raised their tea cups three times as a blessing to the gods and then drank the cup empty. The cups were then immediately refilled with the thick tea, which, because of the special occasion, had more butter than usual — a real treat in Chialsa, where butter is so expensive. Rice was passed around, blessed, and eaten — pressed into balls — by hand.

They prayed for Tibetan independence and for the long life of the Dalai Lama; they prayed for the enlightenment of all sentient beings. As the prayers drew to a close, the settlement manager rose and walked to the front of the altar, bowed his head, and prostrated three times. Chanting, he offered a white scarf and several wrapped parcels to the gods and to the Dalai Lama, then returned to his seat. The refugees formed a line and waited their turn to prostrate before the altar and offer white scarves to the photograph of the Dalai Lama. The worshipers then filed outside into the cool, gray day. Chatting with neighbors, they strolled home to plow their fields in preparation for planting potatoes.

Since the confrontations with the Nepalese government, Tibetans have tried to keep a low profile in Nepal. For some time, they could still demonstrate quietly on Tibetan Uprising Day, even in Kathmandu, as long as the placards, songs, and speeches were only in Tibetan. Since the recent Chinese crackdown on demonstrations in Tibet, however, the refugees' freedom of speech has been even more restricted in Nepal. The Dalai Lama's representative there must choose his words carefully. Tibetan gatherings and celebrations — even religious ones — are being watched more closely.

Recognizing that political activities play an important role in cultural survival, the Dalai Lama also realizes that Tibetans in Nepal have a slightly different but equally important contribution to make to the Tibetan cause:

> I think there is another field in which Tibetans in Nepal can help the Tibetan cause. Tibetans, with Chinese permission, are coming out to see their relatives in India as well as in Nepal. For those people, this is their first step in a free society, a free country like Nepal. Politically, I think it is very important to show, to make them feel, these new Tibetans, what is the value of freedom. You can express anything you want, the freedom of speech, the freedom of thoughts. (Dalai Lama, personal communication 1986)

Since 1965 Tibetans leaving Tibet have no longer been recognized as refugees; they can no longer cross international borders without some kind of papers. For 15 years or so, almost no Tibetans could leave Tibet. Finally, in the early 1980s, China began to relax the restrictions on international travel, letting thousands cross into Nepal and India to attend the Kalachakra Initiation at Bodh Gaya. In order to be eligible for the Chinese passport, however, they must first say they are Chinese citizens. Since the 1987 demonstrations in Tibet, however, travel for Tibetans to Tibet, India, and Nepal has become extremely difficult and has slowed down dramatically. These restrictions have in turn undermined the role for Tibetans in Nepal mentioned by the Dalai Lama.

The trade embargo between Indian and Nepal that began in April 1989 underscores the fragility of the refugees' position in the Hindu kingdom, and any haven they may temporarily find. Rising out of an ongoing struggle by Nepal to assert its independence from India, the embargo was triggered in part by Nepal's purchase of arms from the Chinese government, an action the Tibetan refugees strongly oppose. As the Nepalese government turns to China for assistance, Tibetans may find the terms by which they are allowed to remain in Nepal to be increasingly unacceptable. They may find themselves forced to choose between the security and stability of the lives they have constructed in Nepal and the political stand that they, as refugees, have chosen to take.

Tibetans do not look upon Tibetan Uprising Day demonstrations or Youth Congress activities as a means of winning back Tibetan independence, but they do see political activities as a way of "recharging the ethnic battery" (Nowak 1984:155), of stepping out of their daily concerns to remember what it is they are working for. They consider the opportunity to express themselves politically to be invaluable in transmitting the immediacy of their struggle to the next generation, and are especially concerned about what impact the political limitations in Nepal will have on their children. They fear that without the opportunity to demonstrate actively against the Chinese occupation, their children will gradually lose interest; they will not inherit the sense of urgency, the sense of responsibility that if they do not work for the Tibetan cause, they will have betrayed their country. And thus, these Tibetans fear that, if forced to choose between the concrete security of a home, even a home in another nation, and the insecure adherence to an abstract ideal, refugees born and raised in Nepal may choose the path of security and stability offered by citizenship in another nation.

Epilogue

The tenth of March, 1988, dawned crisp and clear. I caught the 8:35 morning train in Stamford, Connecticut, and settled down to read *The New York Times*. Fifty-five minutes later I arrived in Grand Central Terminal and wove my way through the crowds of gray-suited professionals, elegantly dressed visitors, and homeless people clad in rags. I nodded to the middle-aged Vietnamese man, dressed in a baggy polyester jacket, tentatively holding out fliers for a Rite Aid special on lipstick, and stepped out onto the swarming sidewalks of Manhattan.

Orienting myself amidst the constant motion, I set out across town to the steps of the United Nations building, where a crowd was already gathering. Slogans declaring "Tibetan Independence!" and "Stop Genocide in Tibet!" decorated posterboard signs lining a metal fence. A red silk banner with "Free Tibet" sewn in vibrant, yellow letters was flown by two Tibetans. Carved in stone on the wall behind them was this message: "They shall beat their swords into ploughshares and their spears into pruning hooks/Nations shall not lift up sword against nation/Neither shall they learn way any more" (Isaiah). Volunteers canvassed the UN entrance, distributing flyers describing the genocide and cultural devastation of Tibet by the Chinese. Curious pedestrians stopped to ask questions: Where is Tibet? Exactly what have the Chinese done? Journalists quickly jotted down notes; TV camera operators bobbed around the perimeter.

The group of 300 collected at the base of the steps. Rinchen Dharlo, now representative of the Dalai Lama in New York, faced the crowd and read the speech the Dalai Lama was delivering thousands of miles away in northern India.

> Today we pay special tribute to the courage and determination of the Tibetan people, so many of whom have given their lives for our just and noble cause.

The suffering to which our people have been subjected during these decades mark the darkest period in our history.

The struggle of the Tibetan people is a struggle for our inalienable right to determine our own destiny in freedom. It is a struggle for democracy, human rights and peace. Most of all, it is a struggle for our survival as a people and a nation with a unique civilization. (Dalai Lama 1988:2)

After the address, a tourist to Tibet took the microphone and described the recent bloodshed from the riots in Lhasa. Lastly, the head of the US Tibet Committee updated the crowd on the resolution recently approved by the US Senate condemning human rights violations in Tibet. He encouraged us to keep writing our legislators, to somehow keep the spotlight on Tibet.

Sufficiently buoyed into action, the crowd set out for the Chinese embassy, crying "China Out of Tibet!" "Tibet belongs to Tibetans!" With the help of police who stopped traffic, we wove our way through the lunch throngs of Fifth Avenue. For two short hours, the energy of the crowd was palpable; we believed we could make a difference. Too soon, however, the demonstration came to an end; upcoming events were announced and the crowd began to disperse.

*   *   *   *   *

Unlike many other once-isolated peoples now slipping into the twentieth century, Tibetans are trying to enter by design. Daily they perform unspoken tasks of cultural reconstruction, struggling to save what is essential to their identity while allowing other elements to be torn away by the roughness of modern society. They are seeking to incorporate those parts of the twentieth century that will assist them in achieving their objectives: Tibetans in Washington and New York lobby Congress and the UN; Tibetans everywhere are slowly learning the advantages of working with the media. In this way, they are striving to maintain a balance between isolation and assimilation, between a lack of compromise and a lack of identity. Tibetans repeatedly told me that what their children do, what language they speak, or where they live does not matter; it is essential, however, that these children continue to think of themselves as Tibetan, that they still work for the freedom of their nation.

Expectations raised over the past 10 years have been dashed repeatedly. The fact-finding missions led by Tibetan refugee leaders of the late 1970s and early 1980s have had insignificant political effects. Potential talks between the Dalai Lama and the Chinese were called off in early 1989. In March of that year, the Chinese imposed martial law in Tibet, and in June Chinese leaders imposed martial law on China in its entirety.

It is unlikely that these setbacks will lead the Tibetans inside Tibet to give up hope, to forget the Tibetan cause. These Tibetans have few alternatives. Resisting Chinese domination is their only hope for obtaining the fundamental freedoms for which they yearn as humans. The refugees, however, do have an alternative; they can choose to become citizens of another society and thus obtain the rights and freedoms offered other full members of that society. Thus far, few have chosen this path. Yet how long can children educated and raised in a foreign society continue to care about returning to a homeland in which they have never lived? How long can they be expected to lead lives in limbo, partial participants in the societies in which they live and work? How long can a culture in exile retain the potency and clarity necessary to continue serving as a guide for action and as a motive for sacrifice?

The Dalai Lama embodies Tibetan culture and the Tibetan cause; he provides the refugees with a concrete example of how to live by the abstract values of their culture and of why the sacrifices they are called on to perform are so critical. Moreover, he offers the world an alternative vision for how we can and should act and interact with each other. And he is making the Tibetan struggle for independence our own struggle for a more meaningful life. He writes, "It is in our own interest to create a world of love, justice and equality, for without a sense of universal responsibility based on morality, our existence and survival is at a perilous precipice" (Dalai Lama 1980:109). And later:

> At present the world is suffering from great conflicts. . . . All of these arise from a lack of understanding of one another's human-ness. The answer to them is not an armaments race or a show of force, but an understanding of the common quality [of seeking happiness]. The solution is not technological or political, it is spiritual; a sensitive understanding of our common situation. (Dalai Lama 1980:111)

The Dalai Lama is not calling for recognition of Tibet's rights and freedoms at the expense of those of the Chinese; rather, he is seeking a means by which the interests of both can be recognized and respected. He is calling upon others to join not only the Tibetans' struggle for independence, but in all struggles to obtain justice and equality, in all attempts to create a more humane, a more just world.

The tale of the Tibetan refugees is one of quiet endurance. They are reconstructing their culture and their lives; they are surviving in exile. But they also have a growing sense that their options are more limited, that their time for reaching their goal is running out. More and more Han Chinese are relocated daily to the Tibetan plateau, threatening to outnumber the Tibetans and undermining the Tibetans' claims of nationality. Freedoms throughout China have been brutally and openly repressed in the recent crackdown in Tiananmen Square. The Dalai Lama is aging. Tibetans are reluctant to envision a future without Tenzin Gyatso. His mortality is never discussed. I asked one refugee to describe the Tibetan community in 50 years, under the rule of a 15th Dalai Lama — or no Dalai Lama at all. He stared silently at the ground for a long time. Finally, he said quietly, "It will be very, very difficult."

References

Avedon, J.
    1984   *In Exile from the Land of Snows.* New York: Alfred A. Knopf.

Berbaum, E.
    1980   *The Way to Shambhala.* Garden City, NY: Anchor Press.

Corlin, C.
    1975   The Nation in Your Mind: Continuity and Change Among Tibetan Refugees in Nepal. Ph.D. diss. Goteborg: University of Goteborg.

Cultural Survival Quarterly
    1988   Special Section on Tibet. 12(1):42–76.

Das, C.
    1985   *Tibetan English Dictionary.* New Delhi: Gaurav Publishing House.

Dalai Lama, His Holiness
    1980   *Universal Responsibility and the Good Heart.* Dharmsala: Library of Tibetan Works and Archives.
    1985   Education Conference – June 25-26, 1985. *Tibetan Bulletin* 15(4):4.
    1987   Statement of His Holiness the Dalai Lama on the 28th Anniversary of the Tibetan National Uprising Day. *Tibetan Review,* April.

Dhargyey, Geshe and Geshe Rapten
    1977   *Advice from a Spiritual Friend: Buddhist Thought Transformation.* New Delhi: Publications for Wisdom Culture.

Gold, P.
    1984   *Tibetan Reflections: Life in a Tibetan Refugee Community.* London: Wisdom Publications.

Govinda, A.
    1970   *The Way of the White Clouds.* Boston: Shambhala Publications.

Hagen, T.
    1969   To the History of the Tibetan Refugee Relief Program in Nepal. Kathmandu, Nepal.

Harrer, H.
    1959   *Seven Years in Tibet.* New York: Dutton.

Harris, G. L.
1973   *Area Handbook for Nepal, Bhutan and Sikkim.* Washington, DC: US Government Printing Office.

Hogger, Dr.
1972   Minutes of Constituent General Meeting of the Snow Lion Foundation Meeting, 25 February.

Jamyang Norbu
1979   *Horseman in the Snow: The Story of Aten, an Old Khampa Warrior.* Dharmsala: Information Office, Central Tibetan Secretariat.

Joshi, B.
1983   Report on the History of the Tibetan Refugee Settlement in Nepal: 1961-83. Swiss Association for Technical Assistance (SATA).

Michael, F.
1985   A Nation in Exile: Building an Alternate Tibet. *Tibetan Review,* pp. 21-29.

NITRRC (Nepal International Tibetan Refugee Relief Committee)
1960   Minutes from 7 April.

News Tibet
1988   22(4): 2. New York.

Nowak, M.
1984   *Tibetan Refugees: Youth and the New Generation of Meaning.* New Brunswick, NJ: Rutgers University Press.

SATA (Swiss Association for Technical Assistance)
1965   Working Paper regarding the Aid for Tibetan Refugees in Nepal. Jawalakhel, Nepal. Unpublished document.

Shawcross, W.
1985   *The Quality of Mercy: Cambodia, Holocaust and Modern Conscience.* New York: Simon and Schuster.

Sonam Rapstong
1985   Tibetan Education: Twenty-Five Years in Exile. A publication of the Council of Tibetan Education. New Delhi: Indraprastha Press.

Thurman, R.A.
1985   Tibet: Mystic Nation in Exile. *Parabola.* Summer.

Tibet Society and Relief Fund of the United Kingdom
1985   Report on How to Save the Monasteries. The Tibet Society and Relief Fund of the United Kingdom Report. Spring.

Tibetan Bulletin
1985   Interview with the Dalai Lama: Political Freedom Must for Buddhist Practices. 15(4): 25-26.

1969   *Tibetans in Exile: Ten Years in India.* Compiled by the Office of His Holiness Dalai Lama. New Delhi: Gutenberg Printing Press.

Tucci, G.
1980   *The Religions of Tibet.* Translated by G. Samuel. Berkeley: University of California Press.

Ugen Gombo
    1975   Tibetan Refugees in the Kathmandu Valley: A Study of Socio-Cultural Change and Continuity and the Adaptation of a Population in Exile. Ph.D. diss. Stonybrook: State University of New York.

Weiderkehr, E.
    1974   Letter to Dhundup Namgyal. 6 November.
    n.d.   Letter to Dhundup Namgyal.

About Cultural Survival

Cultural Survival, a nonprofit human rights organization founded in 1972 by social scientists at Harvard University, is concerned with the fate of indigenous peoples and ethnic groups throughout the world. Members include a network of approximately 2,500 anthropologists and other social scientists who have worked with specific groups, particularly indigenous peoples, worldwide. The organization has sponsored and facilitated research on both urgent and chronic issues relating to development and social change in Africa, Latin America and Asia, with a special focus on the general and specific problems confronting indigenous peoples incorporated into encompassing state systems.

Cultural Survival also directly funds projects that are designed and implemented by indigenous peoples themselves to promote their self-sufficiency. This is done with the aim of giving such groups the time and economic resources with which to determine their relation to economic and political systems at the state level.

Cultural Survival often sponsors research, however, on topics in places where it does not have or intend to have in the near future direct assistance projects of its own. One of its purposes as an institution is to make available its own expertise (or the expertise it can rally) to other, larger organizations who either have ongoing programs in areas of concern or have the capacity to launch such programs. Research on the Ethiopian famine fell in line with this latter goal of Cultural Survival.

Research among refugees has become a concern of Cultural Survival in the course of its efforts to protect the rights of indigenous peoples. Racism, discrimination and ethnic persecution in indigenous people's homelands often cause them to cross international borders. Cultural Survival has conducted research among refugees in or from Costa Rica, Djibouti, Ethiopia, Guatemala, Mexico, Nicaragua, Ruanda, Somalia, Sudan and Uganda, and as a result has published numerous documents on the general relationship between ethnicity and refugee status.

Recently, Cultural Survival has begun to evaluate resource management projects run by indigenous peoples and funded by Cultural Survival as well as other organizations.

Cultural Survival publishes and/or distributes more than 350 documents about the plight of indigenous peoples and ethnic minorities throughout the world.

CULTURAL SURVIVAL PUBLICATIONS

CULTURAL SURVIVAL REPORTS

Politics and the Ethiopian Famine, 1984-1985. By Jason W. Clay and Bonnie K. Holcomb. (No. 20, December 1986; revised edition.) 240 pages. $9.95.

Southeast Asian Tribal Groups and Ethnic Minorities. Proceedings of a Cultural Survival-sponsored conference. (No. 22, 1988.) $10.

Coca and Cocaine: Effects on People and Policy in Latin America. Edited by Deborah Pacini and Christine Franquemont. Proceedings of the conference "The Coca Leaf and Its Derivatives — Biology, Society and Policy." Published with the Latin American Studies Program, Cornell University. (No. 23, June 1986.) 169 pages. $8.

Human Rights and Anthropology. Edited by Theodore E. Downing and Gilbert Kushner, with Human Rights Internet. (No. 24, 1988.) 208 pages. $12.

The Spoils of Famine: Ethiopian Famine Policy and Peasant Agriculture. By Jason W. Clay, Bonnie Holcomb, Peter Niggli, and Sandra Steingraber. (No. 25, 1988.) 200 pages. $15.

A Sea of Small Boats. Edited by John Cordell. (No. 26, 1988.) 300 pages. $15.

Indigenous Peoples and Tropical Forests: Models of Land Use and Management from Latin America. By Jason W. Clay. (No. 27, 1988.) 150 pages. $8.

Report from the Frontier: The State of the World's Indigenous Peoples. By Julian Burger. (No. 28, 1987.) 320 pages. $15.

(Cultural Survival Reports continue the Occasional Paper series.)

OCCASIONAL PAPERS

The Chinese Exodus from Vietnam: Implications for the Southeast Asian Chinese. By Judith Strauch. (No. 1, December 1980.) 15 pages. $2.

East Timor: Five Years After the Indonesian Invasion. Statements by M. Alkatiri, R. Clark, J. Dunn, J. Joliffe, Amnesty International, E. Traube and B. R. O'G. Anderson to the Fourth Committee of the U.N. General Assembly; articles by D. Southerland (*The Christian Science Monitor*) and T. Harkin (*The Progressive*). (No. 2, January 1981.) 42 pages. $2.25.

The Cerro Colorado Copper Project and the Guaymí Indians of Panama. By Chris N. Gjording, S. J. (No. 3, March 1981.) 50 pages. $4.

The Akawaio, the Upper Mazaruni Hydroelectric Project, and National Development in Guyana. By William Henningsgaard. (No. 4, June 1981.) 37 pages. $2.

Brazilian Indians Under the Law. Proceedings of a Cultural Survival-sponsored conference of lawyers and anthropologists in Santa Catarina, Brazil, in October 1980. (No. 5, September 1981.) 14 pages. $1.75.

In the Path of Polonoroeste: Endangered Peoples of Western Brazil. Articles by D. Maybury-Lewis, D. Price, D. Moore, C. Junqueira, B. M. Lafer and J. Clay. (No. 6, September 1981.) 66 pages. $4.

The Plight of Peripheral People in Papua New Guinea. Volume I: The Inland Situation. Edited by Robert Gordon. Contributions by J. Flanagan, P. Huber, D. Jorgenson, J.-C. Martin and F.-R. Ouellette, N. L. Maclean, and E. L. Schieffelin. (No. 7, October 1981.) 95 pages. $7.

The Dialectics of Domination in Peru: Native Communities and the Myth of the Vast Amazonian Emptiness. By Richard Chase Smith. (No. 8, October 1982.) 131 pages. $10.

The San in Transition. Volume I: A Guide to "N!ai, the Story of a !Kung Woman." By Toby Alice Volkman. Published with Documentary Education Resources. (No. 9, November 1982.) 56 pages. $4.

Voices of the Survivors. The Massacre at Finca San Francisco, Guatemala. Published with the Anthropology Resource Center. (No. 10, September 1983.) 105 pages. $7.

The Impact of Contact: Two Yanomama Case Studies. By John Saffirio & Raymond Hames, and Napoleon Chagnon & Thomas F. Melancon. Published with Working Papers on South America. (No. 11, November 1983.) 66 pages. $7.

Micronesia as Strategic Colony: The Impact of U.S. Policy on Micronesian Health and Culture. Edited by Catherine Lutz. (No. 12, June 1984.) 109 pages. $8.

The San in Transition, Volume II: What Future for the Ju/Wasi of Nyae-Nyae? By Robert Gordon. (No. 13, July 1984.) 44 pages. $4.

The Eviction of Banyaruanda: The Story Behind the Refugee Crisis in Southwest Uganda. By Jason W. Clay. (No. 14, August 1984.) 77 pages. $6.

Resource Development and Indigenous People: The El Cerrejón Coal Project and the Guajiro of Colombia. By Deborah Pacini Hernandez. (No. 15, November 1984.) 54 pages. $5.

Native Peoples and Economic Development: Six Case Studies from Latin America. Edited by Theodore Macdonald, Jr. (No. 16, December 1984.) 103 pages. $8.

Art, Knowledge and Health: Development and Assessment of a Collaborative Auto-Financed Organization in Eastern Ecuador. By Dorothea S. Whitten and Norman Whitten, Jr. Published with the Sacha Runa Research Foundation. (No. 17, January 1985.) 126 pages. $9.

The Future of Former Foragers in Australia and Southern Africa. Edited by Carmel Schrire and Robert Gordon. (No. 18, October 1985.) 125 pages. $10.

Ethnic Diversity on a Corporate Plantation: Guaymí Labor on a United Brands Subsidiary in Costa Rica and Panama. By Philippe Bourgois. (No. 19, December 1985.) 52 pages. $5.

Strategies and Conditions of Political and Cultural Survival in American Indian Societies. By Duane Champagne. (No. 21, December 1985.) 56 pages. $8.

SPECIAL REPORTS

Brazil. Articles translated from "A Questão de Emancipação" (Comissão Pro-Indio, São Paulo, 1979) and "Nimuendaju" (Comissão Pro-Indio, Rio de Janeiro, 1979). (No. 1, December 1979.) 68 pages. $2.

The Indian Peoples of Paraguay: Their Plight and Their Prospects. By David Maybury-Lewis and James Howe. (No. 2, October 1980.) 122 pages. $4.

Amazonía Ecuatoriana: La Otra Cara del Progresso. Edited by Norman E. Whitten, Jr. Contributions by N. E. Whitten, Jr., E. Salazar, P. Descola, A. C. Taylor, W. Belzner, T. Macdonald, Jr., and D. Whitten. Published with Mundo Shuar. (No. 3, 1981.) 227 pages. $5.

Fishers of Men or Founders of Empire? The Wycliffe Bible Translators in Latin America. A U.S. Evangelical Mission in the Third World. By David Stoll. Published with Zed Press. (No. 4, December 1982.) 344 pages. $12.99.

Add $2 postage and handling charge for all orders of three titles or less. After three titles, add 50¢ for each additional book. Titles not yet published or out of stock will be backordered and shipped as soon as they are available. Please send check or money order for the amount of order to Cultural Survival Publications, 11 Divinity Avenue, Cambridge, MA 02138. Bookstores and those needing publications for classroom use should write for special rates.